The Contemporary Singer

Elements

Anne Peckham

Berklee Press

Director: Dave Kusek
Managing Editor: Debbie Cavalier
Marketing Manager: Ola Frank
Sr. Writer/Editor: Jonathan Feist

ISBN 978-0-87639-107-5

Berklee
Press

1140 Boylston Street
Boston, MA 02215-3693 USA
(617) 747-2146

Visit Berklee Press Online at
www.berkleepress.com

DISTRIBUTED BY

HAL•LEONARD®
7777 W. BLUEMOUND RD. P.O. BOX 13819
MILWAUKEE, WISCONSIN 53213

Visit Hal Leonard Online at
www.halleonard.com

Table of Contents

Performers: Jude Crossen, voice
Tamara Gebhardt, voice
Anne Peckham, voice
David Shrewsbury, piano

LEVEL 1 WORKOUT FOR LOW VOICES

ADVANCED WORKOUT FOR LOW VOICES

DEMONSTRATION TRACKS

THE CONTEMPORARY SINGER discusses the elements of singing, addressing the specific needs of singers of popular music. It is intended for singers of all levels who want to improve their stamina, increase their range, develop a better sound, and enhance their overall vocal health. *The Contemporary Singer* and its audio are the ideal tools for creating a singing course for students of almost any age group, from junior high school to college to professional. ■ Since 1987, I have been teaching voice at Berklee College of Music, where I developed a course called "Elements of Vocal Technique." This book is the result of these efforts and of my teaching experiences.

1 **NOTES ON THE SECOND EDITION**

In this, the second edition of *The Contemporary Singer*, I have included written musical examples of all the exercises on the accompanying recordings. You will be able to see each exercise pattern and the suggested vowel sound or syllable before you sing it. This will enable you to move through the exercises quicker, without first having to wait to hear the demonstration. The range is indicated above each exercise. Notation for the workouts is in appendix D.

The improved *The Contemporary Singer* audio has been remastered so each of the exercises within a workout is separated out into individual tracks, enabling you to locate exercises faster and easily replay them. Each workout is organized similarly, making it easier to keep your place. You will now be able to follow along with the written music too.

All musical examples printed within the chapters are also played as demonstration tracks. These tracks demonstrate specific concepts from the chapters, and therefore are performed only one time through without progressing onward to other keys. Some of these same exercises are also included within the larger vocal workouts, where they move through several keys.

Since I first wrote *The Contemporary Singer*, the language used to describe vocal registers has become more codified. I have included some of the newer science-based explanations of registers. I also have included more information in "Chapter 8, Maintaining Vocal Health." In addition I have included updated and more detailed illustrations of the vocal mechanism.

I hope you enjoy the new features of this edition. Thank you for using *The Contemporary Singer* in your classes and lessons.

Anne Peckham

THANKS TO Sharon Brown, Sean Carberry, Debbie Cavalier, Jonathan Feist, Matt Marvuglio, Yumiko Matsuoka, Donna McElroy, Rick Peckham, Jo-Ann Ross, Jan Shapiro, and Dr. Steven Zeitels.

PART 1

KNOWING YOUR INSTRUMENT

A VOICE IS A COMPLEX INSTRUMENT, capable of a wide range of expression. There are many singers who have a wonderful natural sound without studying singing. However, singers who acquire a vocabulary to describe their vocal mechanism and an understanding of their instrument reap many benefits. You can improve and maintain your vocal sound through years of singing, and learn to prevent and correct problems.

This book will help you learn to take care of your voice and advance your singing to the next level. Studying its techniques will help you understand and develop your voice by describing the basic elements of your instrument and teaching you how to practice. It can help you isolate the physical elements of singing, master them, and then expand this mastery of the details to a more holistic technical and musical whole.

In my teaching experience, I have encountered many myths surrounding vocal training. One myth is that singers of popular music don't need training. Many young singers are surprised to learn that careers of untrained singers can be cut short prematurely due to vocal injuries. Even seasoned performers who have bad habits sometimes must relearn how to sing, or else risk permanent vocal damage.

Music styles such as pop, rock, gospel, country music, and musical theater can involve loud singing for extended periods of time, which can be very tiring to your voice. You might have the added problem of performing in venues that may be dry, dusty, and smoky, and have to project over a background of noise.

Comprehensive voice study will help you develop proper breath management and a resonant tone, improving your voice by building stamina and vocal power. You can learn to minimize vocal tension and understand how your environment affects your voice. Understanding your voice will help you eliminate any bad vocal habits that are holding you back.

Your voice is subject to the effects of your emotions, eating and sleeping habits, use of medications and drugs, and speaking. It is dependent upon your overall good health and vitality. Learning how to take care of your voice and developing good practice habits can help you maintain your singing voice for a lifetime.

Another myth about vocal study is that it leads singers to lose the unique, natural sound of their voices. On the contrary, studying voice can help you build your instrument and enhance its best natural qualities. Mastering the elements of singing, such as breath control, will help you make the most of your natural sound. It will also make you aware of areas that need improvement and habits that are detrimental to vocal longevity. In fact, many successful, professional pop singers take lessons to improve and maintain their voices. Lessons won't make you lose your unique sound. Instead, you will gain control and enhance your instrument.

What is the best vocal method? Every singer explains the complex process of singing differently, using dissimilar terms, and emphasizing different body parts and pedagogical concepts. A good singing method is one that is practical, relevant, has a basis in scientific fact, and uses exercises targeting specific nuts-and-bolts issues for a singer.

Don't be intimidated by technical details when you are learning to sing. Information about your body and voice will help you become a smart singer, knowing how to make the most of your natural instrument.

TIPS FOR GETTING STARTED

■ Focus on long-term goals

As you begin to study voice, keep your long-term goals in mind. Learning to sing is both an intellectual and a physical process. Training your muscles to "remember" how to react when approaching a leap or when sustaining a phrase takes time and practice. You must train your muscles by repeating a task correctly many times so your instrument responds effectively when you perform.

Singers commonly understand technical concepts intellectually long before they are able to perform the skills, so practicing is important. Throughout the process, remember that singing well requires skill. You can develop this through practice and patience. Think positively and acknowledge your successes.

■ Choose your repertoire carefully

Singers need to build a base of positive performance experience in order to develop confidence. Early in vocal development, avoid songs that spotlight your weaknesses. It is better to sing a simple song well than to sing a difficult song poorly. Challenge yourself, but be ready to recognize when you need to put a song away to give your voice the time to develop.

■ Sing for fun

Stay in touch with your love of singing. As you work to improve your singing in practice sessions, make sure you have outlets for performing that are purely pleasurable. Group singing can enhance your joy of making music, so get together with friends, join a choir, and sing for fun. Performing can be very satisfying, even while you work to fulfill your highest potential.

The following overview presents in a nutshell how your voice works. Each of these elements will be described in detail, along with exercises that will develop each specific component of your voice.

AN OVERVIEW OF THE SINGING PROCESS

All musical instruments have three common elements: a generator, a vibrator, and a resonator. Your voice, for example, is powered by breath from your lungs (generator) that makes your vocal folds (vibrator) move. The sound produced by your vocal folds is colored and amplified by resonance in your throat, mouth, and nasal cavity (resonators).

In addition to these three common elements, singers also have *articulators* (the mouth, teeth, tongue, lips, cheeks, and palates) that give singers the unique capability of combining words with music. Skillful articulation is a mark of good vocal technique.

■ Breath (generator)

Air powers your singing, and controlling the inflow and outflow of air requires the skilled use of breathing muscles and organs. These include the trachea, lungs, diaphragm, ribs (and associated muscles), and abdominal muscles.

Many vocal problems originate with these two problems: lack of sufficient breath support, and/or excessive muscular tension. The delicate balance of energy and relaxation is essential to good singing. When you manage your breath well with energy and relaxation, you will see a totally positive effect on your singing. Breath management is one of the most important practices you will learn in vocal study. It affects your intonation, tone quality, sustaining power, range, dynamics, expression, flexibility, phrasing, and stylistic interpretation. This is why good breath management is often the primary focus from the beginning in voice study.

■ Sound production (vibrator)

The larynx is comprised of cartilage, ligaments, muscle, nerves, and mucus membranes. The vocal folds are situated in the larynx and comprised of the arytenoid cartilages, the vocalis muscle (thyroarytenoid), ligaments, and membranes. Activated by the brain with the thought of speaking or singing, nerves control the muscles that close the arytenoid cartilages, bringing the vocal folds together. This closure offers a resistance to airflow, which results in a "buzz tone," the fundamental tone of vocal production.

You can feel your vocal folds vibrating if you place your fingers lightly on the small protrusion at front of your throat (Adam's apple). Say "hoo!" at a moderately high pitch. You will feel a buzzing sensation at your fingers. This is where your vocal folds are.

Your vocal folds do not have nerves that tell you when they need rest or that they are swollen or injured. When you have a sore throat from vocal misuse or illness, you feel the inflammation or infection of surrounding tissues or tired muscles from incorrect singing, not the vocal folds themselves. That is why it is important to listen to your body and stop singing before you get to the point of hoarseness or voice loss.

I had a student years ago who had her upcoming senior recital scheduled when she came down with laryngitis. She could make sound but was very hoarse. She was very anxious to finish her college work so she could start a singing job after graduation. She insisted on singing her recital despite admonishments from her laryngologist and me. A couple of weeks later, she called me from her home, just having been diagnosed with vocal nodules caused by singing with laryngitis. She lost her gig because she couldn't sing, was put on vocal rest for a time (no singing), and then gradually began to recover her voice with voice therapy and much work. This singer could have avoided developing nodules that seriously impaired and set back her singing by resting her voice when she had laryngitis.

■ Resonance (tone enhancer)

The throat, mouth, and nasal cavity are all parts of the vocal tract. The buzz produced by the vibrating vocal folds (the fundamental tone) reverberates in the resonators and enhances the tone. This resonance colors and amplifies tone.

When I work with young men who want to sing rock, they often ask how to get a more powerful sound on high notes. A powerful sound can be developed with energetic breath support, and an awareness of resonance, taking into account variables, such as age and voice type, which will affect your sound output. It is tough for young singers to have the patience to wait to grow into their voices, but it is important to approach your vocal development like an athlete. Runners don't train for a marathon in a week, or in a semester. Learning to sing is a long-term commitment to becoming the best that you can be.

■ Words (articulators)

The tongue, jaw, cheeks, teeth, lips, and palates coordinate to produce speech sounds. Adding words to music makes your voice a unique musical instrument.

Some of my students who are nonnative English speakers must work hard to produce natural sounding English diction. As their pronunciation becomes more smooth and clear, their singing tone often becomes more relaxed and natural as a result.

All basic elements of tone production are interconnected, and mastering them in order to sing freely is the goal of understanding the singing process.

Cross-section of upper body

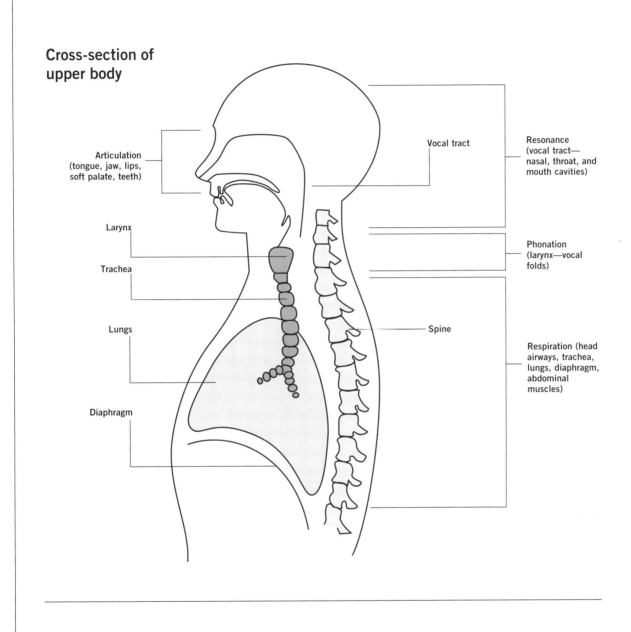

Articulation (tongue, jaw, lips, soft palate, teeth)

Larynx

Trachea

Lungs

Diaphragm

Vocal tract

Resonance (vocal tract— nasal, throat, and mouth cavities)

Phonation (larynx—vocal folds)

Spine

Respiration (head airways, trachea, lungs, diaphragm, abdominal muscles)

9

**Y**OUR VOICE IS A WIND INSTRUMENT that needs breath to produce sound. Training your body and unconscious mind to manage the breathing process will give you the control you need to sing longer phrases, to sing high and low notes well, and to gain better control over dynamics.

POSTURE

Good posture is the first step to making your body work for you because it provides alignment that maximizes lung capacity and releases tension. But posture that feels "natural" to you, even if relaxed, may not provide a high enough chest position for effective singing. You may need to learn what it feels like to stand with correct posture. A collapsed chest makes it difficult to control breath when singing, and it diminishes breathing capacity.

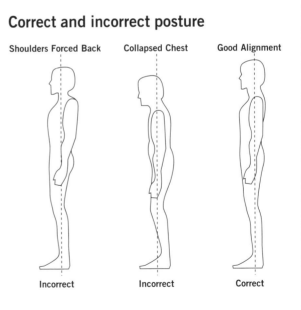

Correct and incorrect posture

Shoulders Forced Back   Collapsed Chest   Good Alignment

Incorrect   Incorrect   Correct

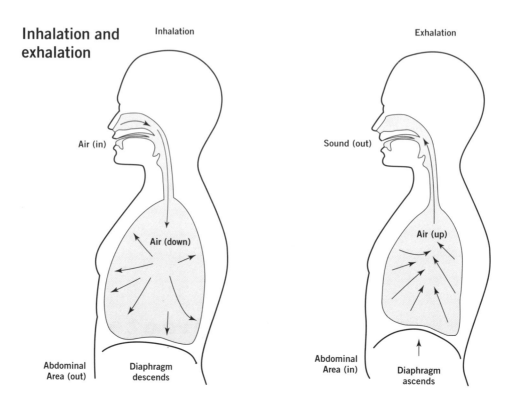

Inhalation and exhalation

Inhalation

Air (in)

Air (down)

Abdominal Area (out)

Diaphragm descends

Exhalation

Sound (out)

Air (up)

Abdominal Area (in)

Diaphragm ascends

To establish good posture, start with a comfortably high chest, relaxed knees (not locked), and feet hip-distance apart. As you become familiar with good posture it will feel more natural to you. During singing, be sure to keep your chest comfortably high. Beginners should practice while standing in front of a mirror because it is easier to see good posture than to feel it, when you are starting out.

Singers of pop and rock music sometimes resist good posture habits because they are afraid of appearing formal or "classical." But since contemporary music can be strenuous to voices, it is especially these singers who need good posture to reduce tension and increase breath capacity. If you do not actively involve your body in breath support, you will be more likely to strain or injure your vocal folds.

■ **Moving while singing**

Singers need to be able to manage their breath without actively thinking about it so they can focus their energy on performing. Experienced performers can sing while vigorously dancing and in almost any position, including lying down. While you are training your voice, however, correct posture allows you to focus on breath management and helps free tone production.

Begin by working on breath management while standing still and looking in a mirror. Once you understand the concepts and master the physical coordination, movement will not compromise your singing. Practicing makes correct breathing natural and automatic, so that you don't always have to think about it. Of course, to sing and move without becoming winded, you must be in good physical condition, which may require maintaining a regular exercise routine.

■ **Everyday breath vs. singing breath**

Breathing as an automatic, natural function is usually taken for granted. Singing, however, requires deep, relaxed breathing that has been refined to minimize tension and maximize efficiency. Studying the respiratory mechanism and the way it functions will help you master your breathing.

FOUR STEPS OF EFFECTIVE BREATHING

Try this simple exercise that outlines four steps of the breathing process.

1. Align your body.

2. Inhale and expand around your waistline.

3. Exhale with firm abdominals.

4. Keep ribs and chest open and stable as you exhale (sing).

14

When inhaling, don't overfill your lungs. Stuffing your lungs creates tension in your throat and jaw before you even make a sound. Inhale completely by expanding around your waistline and in your lower abdominal area, taking care not to create tension by lifting your shoulders.

■ Practice makes perfect

Singers, like athletes, must develop physical skills in order to perform well.

Almost anyone can run, but athletes train to run a marathon. In the same way, you are training to use your breath in a more demanding way than the average person does, developing special skills the non-singer does not need. Moreover, breath management and tone quality are interconnected, so if you want to improve your tone, work on breath management.

The diaphragm

The *diaphragm* is a flat muscle, curved in a double-dome shape, separating the chest cavity from the abdominal cavity. It connects to the bottom of your ribs and is the floor of your rib cage.

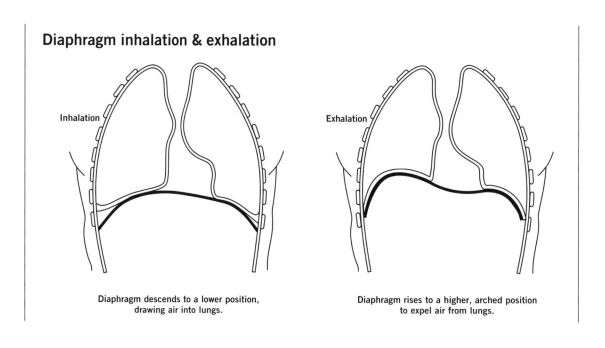

Diaphragm inhalation & exhalation

Inhalation

Exhalation

Diaphragm descends to a lower position,
drawing air into lungs.

Diaphragm rises to a higher, arched position
to expel air from lungs.

In a relaxed position, your diaphragm is slightly arched upward. When you expand your midsection by relaxing your abdominal muscles, your diaphragm descends into a more flattened position, creating a vacuum in your lungs that causes air to rush in. During exhalation, your firm abdominal muscles cause the diaphragm to arch upward in a double-dome shape and expel air. Your diaphragm is not consciously controlled during singing, but rather moves with its associated rib and abdominal muscles.

Most people have the erroneous idea that the diaphragm is located in the same position as the abdominal muscles, across the front of the belly. The instruction to "sing from your diaphragm" accompanied by a pat on your tummy may direct your attention to the right general area, but is misleading as to where your diaphragm is actually located. In fact, it is positioned horizontally inside your body and cannot be felt by placing your hand on your belly. You can find the general location of your diaphragm by feeling along the bottom of your rib cage and imagine that it is inside your body, under your ribs in the position of an upside-down bowl.

■ Ribs and lungs

Your rib cage is comprised of bone and cartilage. During breathing, the attached intercostal muscles open and close your rib cage, filling and emptying your lungs. The external intercostals expand your rib cage during a full breath, while the internal intercostals force air out during exhalation. Singers try to resist the contraction of the internal intercostals to avoid running out of air. When you sing, steady flow of air to your vocal folds is achieved by opening your ribs and slightly contracting your abdominal muscles.

This exercise will help increase your awareness of the expansion of your rib cage.

1. Place your fists on your sides above your waist.

2. Take a full breath and feel the expansion of your rib cage.

3. Exhale and feel your rib cage become narrow.

4. Take a second breath, spreading your ribs as wide as you can. Try to not lift your shoulders.

5. Hold your breath but keep your throat open. Slowly, count to four. Maintain an open rib cage as you hold your breath. You will feel the external intercostal muscles of your ribs working to stay open.

6. Exhale and allow your ribs to become narrow again.

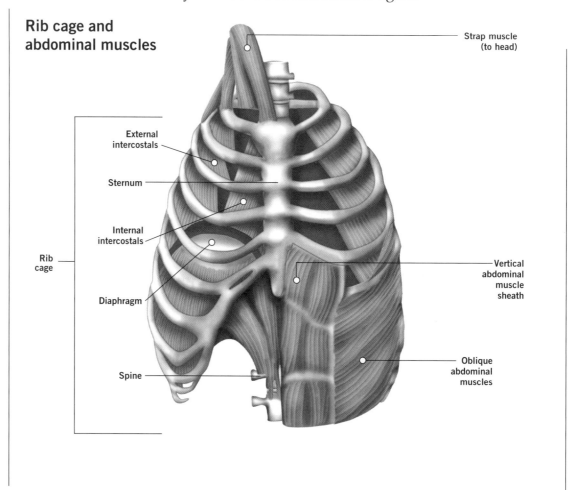

Rib cage and abdominal muscles

Strap muscle (to head)

External intercostals

Sternum

Internal intercostals

Rib cage

Diaphragm

Spine

Vertical abdominal muscle sheath

Oblique abdominal muscles

■ The abdominal muscles

These powerful muscles cover the entire abdominal region running vertically and diagonally across your belly. Your lower abdominal muscles relax outward during inhalation and contract inward slightly during exhalation.

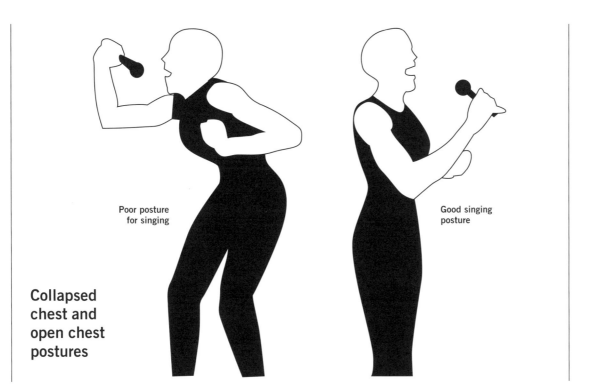

Poor posture
for singing

Good singing
posture

**Collapsed
chest and
open chest
postures**

During singing, your rib cage should stay open while your abdominal muscles move in slightly. This is called *support*; it enables your diaphragm to ascend to its high position at a slower rate, allowing you to sustain longer phrases and maintain better pitch control. If your ribs descend immediately, air will rush out too quickly for good phrasing, or a breathy tone may result. Collapsing your ribs and chest tightens your neck and throat muscles, preventing your larynx from functioning freely. This can cause your singing to sound and feel constricted.

DIFFERENT APPROACHES TO BREATHING

There are three main ways that singers tend to breathe, but only one of them is widely considered to be effective. The others can lead to poor intonation (singing out of tune), lack of sustaining power, poor tone quality, and a host of other vocal problems. In fact, many vocal problems are rooted in either inadequate breath support or excessive muscular tension caused by chest breathing or rib breathing.

■ **Chest breathing** (very limited effectiveness)

Chest breathing involves raising the shoulders and chest for inhalation and lowering the chest for exhalation. While this allows air to move in and out very quickly, singers should not use this technique because it is difficult to control the airflow for phrasing, and the pumping motion of the chest and shoulders creates tension. When your neck and shoulder muscles are tight, the internal muscles of the larynx cannot function freely. This kind of breathing can produce tone that is overly breathy, strained, weak, and out of tune.

■ **Rib breathing** (somewhat limited effectiveness)

Rib breathing involves expansion in the ribs, but not the lower abdominal muscles. Some singers tend to breathe this way to maintain a trim profile or because of admonitions from classical ballet training to hold in the tummy or to "pull up." Others have not developed the awareness required to release these muscles. Also, some singers have highly developed abdominal muscles that are difficult to relax outward during inhalation. Because contracted abdominal muscles restrict full inhalation, rib breathing is not recommended for singing. Rib breathing can lead to lack of sustaining power and throat tension, and can revert to chest breathing.

■ **Rib/abdominal breathing** (most effective)

The most effective breathing method for singers is rib breathing combined with relaxation of your low abdominal muscles during inhalation. Relaxed abdominal muscles allow you take a full breath, and minimize throat and neck tension during exhalation. Your lower abdominal muscles contract slightly as you exhale working in opposition to your diaphragm, which is controlled by keeping your rib cage open. When your rib muscles, diaphragm, and abdominal muscles control the work of breath support, your larynx can function without interference from its surrounding muscles.

BREATHING EXERCISES

■ Breath observation

This exercise is helpful in encouraging proper abdominal action in singing. Simply observe your body's natural movement and don't try to do anything special to influence your breathing.

1. Lay on the floor and place a small book approximately 1 1/2 inches thick under your head to align your body.

2. Focus your attention on your natural breathing process. As you inhale, your abdominal muscles below your rib cage rise, and as you exhale, they move inward. Observe the openness of your ribs around your waistline and memorize this feeling.

3. Rest your hands on your abdomen and breathe normally, observing the rise and fall of your belly.

4. Stand up and reproduce this breathing action, expanding as you inhale.

■ Releasing abdominal muscles

This is especially useful for singers who need to become aware of how to release their lower abdominal muscles to take a full breath.

1. Stand with your feet about 18 inches away from a table (or the back of a chair).

2. Lean with your hands on the edge, as if you were looking at something on the table.

3. Take a slow, deep breath, letting your belly feel as if it will fall toward the floor. Don't hold your abdominal muscles in, but rather allow them to drop, assisted by gravity.

4. Exhale, with firm abdominal muscles.

THE CONTEMPORARY SINGER

20

ELEMENTS OF VOCAL TECHNIQUE

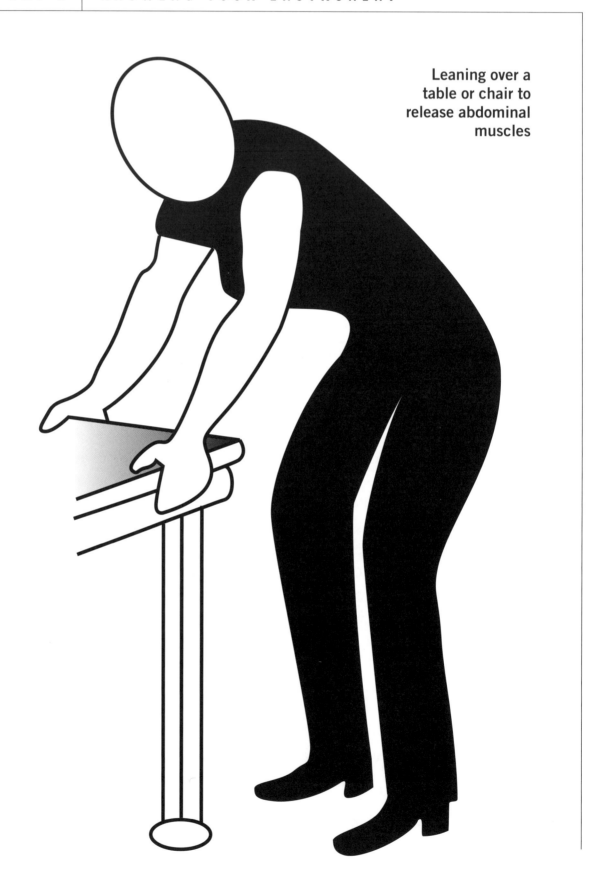

Leaning over a
table or chair to
release abdominal
muscles

5. Inhale again, feeling the expansion in your back muscles and the release of your abdominal muscles toward the floor.

6. Try singing a few easy passages of a song, letting your abdominal muscles drop toward the floor when you inhale between phrases.

7. Stand upright and try to get the same released feeling in your abdominal muscles when you inhale.

■ Extending your breath

This exercise can help coordinate and energize your breath support. Practice Step One until you can make it through comfortably, then add on Step Two, then Step Three. Take care not to inhale too fast or raise your chest when you inhale. During the exhalation phase of each step, try to maintain the openness in your ribs for the entire count. When all three steps can be performed consecutively without stopping, increase the exhalation count to 25 or 30. Put your metronome on 80 beats per minute.

Step One

1. Inhale to a count of 10, taking in two tiny sips of air per metronome beat, expanding your lower abdominal muscles and ribs.

   Exhale for 20 beats using repeated short hisses, two hisses per metronome beat. After 20 counts, begin the next inhalation.

2. Inhale again to a count of 10, taking in two tiny sips of air per metronome beat.

   Exhale for 20 beats using one long, sustained hiss.

3. Inhale again to a count of 10, taking in two tiny sips of air per metronome beat.

   Sing "ah" on a comfortable pitch for 20 beats. Try to maintain the feeling of openness in your ribs for the entire exhalation. (Continue without stopping to Step Two if you successfully complete this with no problem.)

Step Two

1. Inhale to a count to 10, taking in one long, continuous, slow breath.

   Exhale for 20 beats using repeated short hisses, two hisses per metronome beat. Inhale the same way to a count of 10 in a slow, continuous sip.

2. Inhale again to a count of 10 in a slow, continuous sip.

   Exhale in a slow continuous hiss to a count of 20.

3. Inhale again to a count of 10 in a slow, continuous sip.

   Sing "ah" on a comfortable pitch for 20 beats. Try to maintain the feeling of openness in your ribs for the entire exhalation. (Continue without stopping to Step Three if you successfully complete the first two steps.)

Step Three

1. Inhale in a quick catch breath in one count.

   Exhale for 20 beats using repeated short hisses, two hisses per metronome beat.

2. Inhale in a quick catch breath in one count.

   Exhale for 20 beats in a continuous hiss.

3. Inhale in a quick catch breath in one count.

   Sing "ah" for 20 beats.

WHEN YOU BREATHE, your vocal folds open and allow air to pass through without resistance. During singing, your closed vocal folds resist the air being expelled, which causes them to vibrate in a fluttering motion. This initiates the process of vocal sound production, or phonation.

To demonstrate the action of your vocal folds during singing, vibrate your lips in a lip trill.[1] Begin by blowing air out and making a bubbling sound with your lips. Then add vocal sound to the lip trill. If your jaw is loose, your lips somewhat moist, and your breath flow constant, you will probably be able to trill your lips consistently. Now, think about the action of your vocal folds. If there is no intruding tension from surrounding muscles, your vocal folds are adequately lubricated, and breath flow is constant, you will probably be able to vocalize throughout your range.

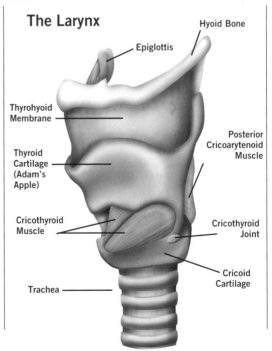

The Larynx

- Hyoid Bone
- Epiglottis
- Thyrohyoid Membrane
- Thyroid Cartilage (Adam's Apple)
- Posterior Cricoarytenoid Muscle
- Cricothyroid Muscle
- Cricothyroid Joint
- Cricoid Cartilage
- Trachea

[1] *If you have tried repeatedly and cannot make this trilling sound, you can do this demonstration by placing your tongue between your lips and blowing.*

Your vocal folds are located in your larynx (voice box), which is comprised of intrinsic (internal), and extrinsic (external) muscles, cartilage, and bone. Your larynx is located at the top of your trachea (windpipe), a cartilaginous tube through which air passes to and from your lungs.

The larynx is suspended in place in the neck by a complex series of muscles commonly referred to as strap muscles. These muscles are capable of influencing sound by elevating or lowering the larynx. Undue tensions in these muscles caused by poor vocal technique can adversely affect the quality of your vocal tone.

The system of nerves that controls all the muscles of the larynx is the most complex in the human body. Your brain controls the action of this complex system automatically. Thinking of speaking or singing coordinates all of the nerves and muscles in the larynx to respond accordingly. Then with adequate air pressure provided by the respiratory system, your vocal folds vibrate, producing sound.

ANATOMY

The outer structure of the larynx is comprised of three major parts: the hyoid bone, the thyroid cartilage, and the cricoid cartilage. (See diagram on p. 23.)

The *hyoid bone*, located at the top of the larynx, is the only actual bone. The protruding bump at the front of the throat (Adam's apple) is the front part of the *thyroid cartilage*. The thyroid cartilage is larger and more prominent in men than in women. The cricoid cartilage, at the bottom of the larynx, connects the voice box to the trachea.

Looking down into the larynx from above is a flap-like cartilage called the epiglottis, which prevents food and liquid from going down the trachea into the lungs.

The *arytenoid cartilages* are positioned on top of the back of the cricoid cartilage with a flexible joint that enables complex motion. The arytenoid cartilages open and close during breathing and phonation, and are involved in changing pitches.

The vocal folds are quite small. They stretch across an opening about the size of a nickel in men, a dime in women. This may help you understand more clearly the delicate nature of your instrument, as well as put its size in perspective when looking at illustrations or videos. Vocal folds can look deceptively large in print or on a television screen.

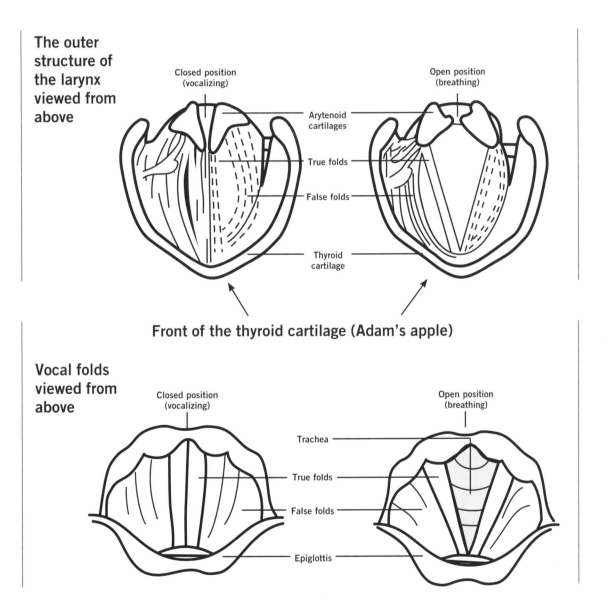

The outer structure of the larynx viewed from above

Closed position (vocalizing)

Open position (breathing)

Arytenoid cartilages

True folds

False folds

Thyroid cartilage

Front of the thyroid cartilage (Adam's apple)

Vocal folds viewed from above

Closed position (vocalizing)

Open position (breathing)

Trachea

True folds

False folds

Epiglottis

INITIATING TONE

There are several ways to initiate a tone, with style, dramatic interpretation, and lyrics all playing a role in how this is accomplished. If a phrase begins with a vowel, or the drama of a song calls for an explosive onset, a singer might begin with a glottal (hard) onset. Other expressions might begin with an aspirate (breathy) onset. But for most singing, the most efficient way to initiate tone is a coordinated (clean) onset.

A *glottal attack* is an explosive onset of tone produced when air pressure is built up under closed vocal folds and suddenly released with a popping sound. In spoken English, this commonly occurs in words that start with vowels. Speak the phrase, "I ate an apple," separating each word with a small, gentle pop. Now, contrast the glottal attack by connecting the end of each word to the beginning of the next, as well as elongating the vowel sounds. This should sound like, "I yea ta napple."

Generally speaking, excessive use of the glottal attack is tiring to your vocal folds and should be avoided unless it's needed for clarity in pronunciation. Singers who tend to use glottal attacks can soften them by adding a very slight H at the beginning of words that start with vowels, and as the attack becomes softer, begin to think the H sound without actually pronouncing it.

Aspirate or *breathy onsets* are characterized by an H sound preceding words that begin with vowels. A breathy attack sounds like "(h)I (h)ate (h)an (h)apple." Although this type of attack is not necessarily hard on your voice, it is not an efficient way to use your breath and can adversely affect the intelligibility of lyrics.

In a coordinated onset, a singer initiates tone in a balanced manner, starting with breath and voice together for a clean beginning without harshness or breathiness. The following exercise can help singers learn to coordinate the starting and stopping of breath and tone. Repeat each exercise moving up by half steps.

Balanced Onset Exercises

 57 *Example 3.1*

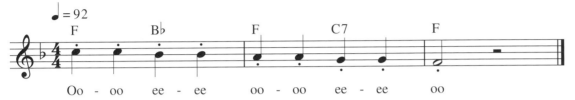

 58 *Example 3.2*

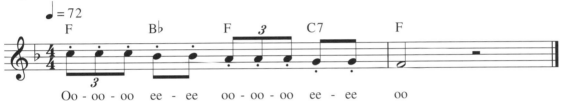

T IMBRE REFERS TO TONE quality in music. Acoustically, tone quality is comprised of two parts: the fundamental tone (the lowest possible frequency of a tone) and higher frequency harmonic overtones. The vibrator (vocal folds) creates the fundamental tone, and harmonic overtones are produced when this vibration sets air molecules in the resonators in motion. A resonant voice rings because harmonic overtones in the human resonators color and amplify the fundamental tone.

Tone quality can be described in terms of "tone colors," such as bright, dark, warm, clear, or brilliant. *Chiaroscuro* is an Italian word used to describe timbre that has both dark and bright characteristics. Because it has richness and brilliance, this kind of tone is thought of as well balanced.

The resonating system of the human voice contains a complex series of air-containing spaces in the head and neck called the *vocal tract*. The size, shape, and aperture of individual cavities affect tone quality, as does the texture of each resonator. Understanding how your resonating system works will help you broaden your range of vocal colors and sing more expressively. Awareness of how proper resonance feels and sounds will help your voice carry better and flow easier.

Profile of vocal tract

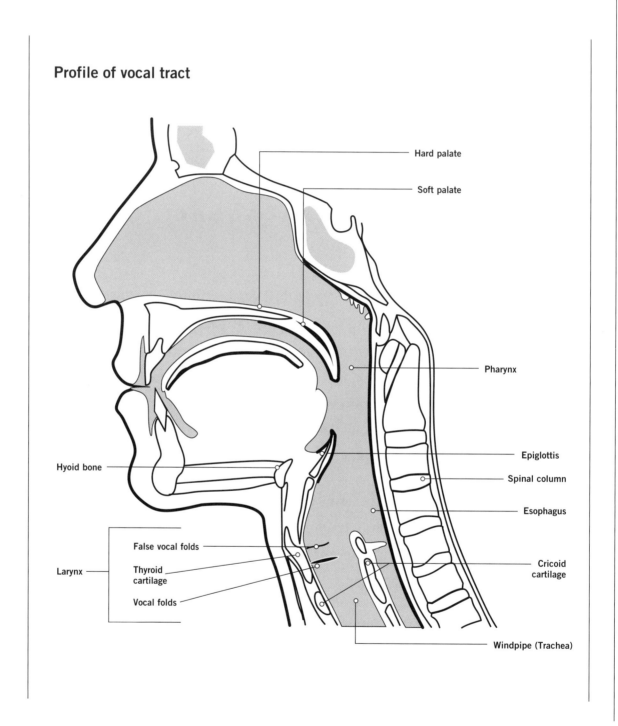

Hard palate

Soft palate

Pharynx

Epiglottis

Spinal column

Esophagus

Hyoid bone

False vocal folds

Larynx

Thyroid cartilage

Vocal folds

Cricoid cartilage

Windpipe (Trachea)

THE RESONATORS

Your vocal sound is a result of many factors, including familial, social, and regional influences, and also the size and shape of your larynx and vocal tract. Because every person's physical makeup and influences are different, your vocal sound is unique to you. The resonators that create your individual vocal sound are discussed below.

■ The pharynx and mouth

The pharynx, typically referred to as the "throat," consists of the area behind the nasal cavity (nasopharynx), mouth (oropharynx), and larynx (laryngopharynx). The nasopharynx is the passage from the back of your nasal cavity to your throat. The oropharynx is the back of your throat that you see when you open your mouth looking in a mirror, while the laryngopharynx is the gateway to the esophagus, the food tube leading to your stomach. The pharynx and the mouth are flexible and together form your largest resonating cavities. You can affect your sound quality by changing the size and shape of your mouth using your jaw, cheeks, lips, and tongue. The pharynx also affects tone because it is muscular and flexible.

■ The chest

The chest is not an efficient resonator because it contains many organs, and the composition of its tissues makes it absorb sound. The vibrations you feel when singing in a low range or at a high volume are thought to be vibrations that actually originate in the laryngopharynx.

■ The larynx

Just above the vocal folds are two small folds called the false vocal folds. In normal singing and speaking, the false vocal folds do not vibrate to make sound. There is a space between the true and false vocal folds called the ventricle, which is thought to be a small, but important resonator.

■ The nasal cavity

The nasal cavity produces a very distinct feeling of vibration when your voice is freely produced. It is thought that the vibrations felt in the nasal cavity actually originate in the nasopharynx.

DISCOVERING YOUR RESONANCE

Resonant tone has carrying power and a clear, ringing sound. In popular music you will hear all kinds of vocal colors used, such as brightness, warmth, breathiness, or clarity. It is helpful to be able to sing with different tone colors at times in popular music. Learning to maximize your resonance will help you discover the bright tone colors of your instrument. Once you have the capability to sing with a clear tone, you can always choose to not use it. If you develop a clear, resonant tone first, then using an occasional breathy tone will be easy.

Remember that you do not hear yourself as others hear you. You hear your own voice vibrating inside your head, while others hear your voice conducted through the air. You can develop a resonant tone by increasing your awareness of how resonance feels, and an awareness of how it should sound by recording yourself.

■ Feeling your tone resonate

To feel your tone resonating, hum a moderately high note and notice the vibrations behind your eyes, cheeks, forehead, lips, and roof of your mouth (hard palate). These combined areas are sometimes referred to as your mask. You might also feel vibrations in your chest or other parts of your body, depending on the volume, pitch, and vowel sound you are singing.

If your voice is resonating well, it will feel comfortable. Any sensation of tickling in the throat, tightness, or pain indicates there is something wrong. Excess tension will interfere with tone and prevent it from resonating freely. Tone that does not resonate efficiently takes more effort to produce. This extra effort causes tension and makes singing laborious and tiring.

If your voice is resonating well, it will feel flexible. A free tone is more likely to resonate well. The tone should feel as if it could go up or down in pitch, be louder or softer, or change to a darker or brighter color. If you feel "stuck" on a note, or your throat feels closed, tension is probably interfering with good resonance.

If your voice is resonating well, it will feel "*buzzy*," as sympathetic vibrations of your voice create a feeling of buzzing in your mask. The intensity of vibrations you feel may depend on the part of your range and the vowel you are singing. Voiced consonants such as Z, M, or N, or closed vowels such as ee and eh, are more likely to cause a distinct feeling of vibration in the lips, nose, and mask. Open vowels such as ah and oh may take more practice to discover the correct resonant feeling.

■ Hearing your tone resonate

The best way to hear that your voice is resonating well is to record yourself singing. If you record yourself singing, you may notice a bell-like "ping" or ringing quality in the sound of your voice on certain pitches or vowels. The brilliance of a resonant voice can augment tonal colors and can be used to convey intense emotions.

A resonant voice sounds as if it flows without tightness in the throat and neck muscles. Efficient use of resonance can help you increase volume without force. In other words, if your voice is resonating well, you do not have to use force to create volume.

A resonant voice sounds in tune. Your ability to match pitches accurately is affected by resonance. A tone that does not resonate well can lack overtones, making pitch sound flat.

■ Imagining

"Placing the tone" refers to a mental concept in which you imagine your tone resonating, usually in a more forward position in the mask. Try to avoid physically manipulating your voice when you are striving for better resonance; this may cause unnecessary tension that works against the resonance you are trying to increase.

Discovering your resonance means experimenting with imagery that sparks your understanding and leads you to progress. Try this imagery and see what works for you.

1. Imagine that the tone continually vibrates on your front teeth. This may help you to discover a way to create brilliant tone without using physical manipulation.

2. Mentally focus on the lyrics of your song to transmit emotional energy. If you are focusing on expressing the spirit of the song and become committed to that expression, you can clear emotional blocks. Emotional blocks can create physical tension that hinders resonant tone.

3. Imagine that you are smiling inside your mouth. The "inner smile" is an image commonly used to help singers raise their soft palates, which increases the open space in the pharynx where tone resonates.

The following exercises are intended to increase your awareness of resonance. Repeat the patterns moving up by half steps.

Resonance Exercise 1

Glide quickly from the mee to the yah sound to feel your tone vibrating in a forward position in your mouth. It will almost sound as if you are singing, "meow," like a cat.

59, 4 *Example 4.1*

Meeyah,   meeyah,   meeyah,   meeyah,   meeyah.

Resonance Exercise 2

Sing the ng with the back of your tongue close to your soft palate, keeping your mouth open. Feel where the tone vibrates on the ng and open to the ah, imagining that your tone vibrates in the same place.

60, 8 *Example 4.2*

(Hu)ng   ah

VOCAL REGISTER is a series of consecutive pitches that have a similar tone quality and are produced using the same muscular actions of the vocal mechanism. Some singers have naturally seamless voices with little or no obvious register changes, while others have extreme tone quality changes in each register.

Registers can be likened to gears in a car transmission, with first gear being your lowest register. As you sing an ascending scale you will probably reach a point where you have to shift gears or registers. This switching of gears in a voice is an adjustment in muscular action, which usually occurs automatically if it is not forced. As you shift registers, you may notice a distinct change in tone quality or that your transitions are not completely smooth even if you aren't forcing. Just as shifting gears smoothly in a manual transmission takes coordination and practice, changing registers smoothly in singing requires muscular coordination and practice.

Blending is a method of training your voice to coordinate through the transitions of your range easily without obvious shifting sounds. Blending can be achieved by working on a combination of breath support and range exercises that employ legato movement between notes.

Weak transitions or weak upper or lower registers can be strengthened with practice. It is extremely helpful to work on these issues with a voice teacher who can help you find appropriate exercises to strengthen and correct any problems.

Blending Exercises

Try these descending exercises to experiment with blending your registers. In each exercise, move smoothly from note to note. Lighten and become softer as you descend. Repeat the patterns, moving up by half steps.

 61 *Example 5.1*

 **62** *Example 5.2*

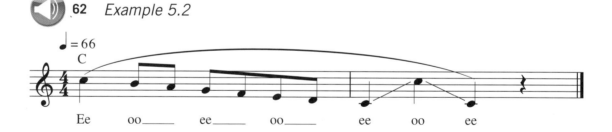

 **63** *Example 5.3*

64, 23   *Example 5.4*

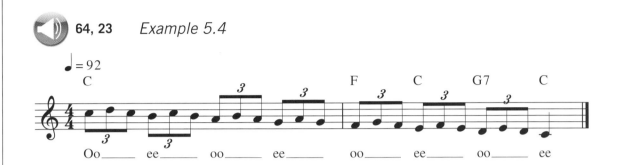

Vocal Registers

Two main muscle actions are responsible for vocal fold activity: the thyroarytenoid muscles and the cricothyroid muscles. The *thyroarytenoid* (TA) muscles are responsible for shortening and thickening the vocal folds. The resulting sound is known as chest voice for both men and women. The *cricothyroid* (CT) muscles are responsible for lengthening and thinning the vocal folds. The resulting sound is known as *head voice* for women and *falsetto* for men. The vocal folds are continuously changing based on pitch, loudness, and resonance.

Mixed or *middle voice* is a term traditionally used to denote a coordinated use of both the thyroarytenoid muscles and the cricothyroid muscles. Even though both muscle groups are active, the mix is TA-dominant. Women frequently employ this mix in singing different styles of contemporary music. Men mix to achieve a blend before transitioning to falsetto. A good middle voice mix can vary in intensity to include a wide range of lighter and more intense TA-dominant tone qualities.

The transitional passage between registers is sometimes called the *passaggio*. Singers also refer to these areas as "breaks." Skilled singers are in control of their voices so their voices don't shift unexpectedly. This desirable blend is achieved by developing muscular coordination, and by adjusting the shape of vowels to keep the voice clear and ringing.

REGISTERS, RANGE, RESONANCE, AND PLACEMENT

The terms *register*, *resonance*, *range*, and *placement* are traditionally used in voice teaching, but are commonly confused and sometimes used inappropriately. Although they are all related to voice production, they refer to entirely different elements. To clarify:

A *vocal register* has a consecutive series of notes that have a similar tone quality and that are produced with consistent muscle action. (See the explanation of different types of registers above).

Range refers to the total scope of notes one can sing.

Resonance is the intensification of a fundamental tone through sympathetic vibration. The fundamental tone is produced by the vocal folds. That buzzing is amplified and colored (intensified) when the vibration of the vocal folds resonates in the air containing spaces of the mouth and throat.

Placement is a concept wherein we imagine focusing the voice's vibrations in different places (on the lips, on the cheek bones, etc.) in order to clarify tone, or to change the color or the quality of the tone.

YODELING

Exaggerating the change between registers to create a flipping sound is a vocal embellishment called *yodeling*, which has been long popular in country music and is now used in pop music as well. A singer who yodels makes a quick, obvious switch from TA-dominant production to CT-dominant production (e.g., listen to Leann Rimes' song "Blue" from the same-titled 1996 album).

Smooth register transitions, however, are used for most styles of music including a variety of popular music, jazz, and musical theater. If you have a natural seamless sound to your voice, enjoy your voice's natural advantage of easy register transitions.

Whether or not a singer naturally has obvious changes between registers varies from person to person. However, most singers will eventually need to learn how to transition into CT-dominant singing (head voice) without breaking.

Blending and strengthening your voice is a long-term project that will require time and practice. Quick-fix solutions for smoothing register transitions are usually temporary and will not establish a reliable technique that holds up in performing situations.

TIPS FOR WORKING ON REGISTERS

1. Use your upper register even if the transition is not smooth. Transitions can be smoothed out with practice. CT-dominant production is a large portion of most women's ranges; for men it is smaller, but equally as important. Accessing and strengthening your upper register makes more range and tone color available to you.

2. Exercises with descending pitch patterns can be helpful in blurring the lines between registers. They also make it easier to pass into a lower register.

3. Exercising your upper register can help improve the quality of your middle and lower range by increasing flexibility, and creating a sense of fearlessness about high notes.

4. Sliding exercises can help induce laryngeal relaxation making register transitions easier.

5. High notes: use them or lose them. As with any physical activity, if you don't do it regularly, you will lose muscle tone. The same is true for singing in your upper register. Voices tend to settle lower and become

heavier and sluggish if they are not exercised throughout the entire range.

6. Vocalize at least one whole step higher than you plan to sing in public. Psychologically, it produces a sense of empowerment and positive attitude to know you could sing a step higher if you had to. Physically, high notes need overtones to make them sound in tune and not forced or screamed. Your highest notes in performances will vibrate with overtones and sound more relaxed and in tune if you exercise your voice higher than you plan to sing in public.

BELTING

Belting is a singing style with a TA-dominant production that is loud, full, and emotional sounding. Belting in both men and women is produced by TA-dominant vocal fold activity. However, the CT muscle must remain active to prevent the vocal folds from over thickening, which produces a heavy vocal fold posture that can cause vocal strain. Research in vocal physiology tells us that specific muscles are responsible for certain sounds: TA-dominant—chest, belt, mix; CT-dominant—head, flute voice, falsetto.

All male singers (except pop and classical countertenors) sing with a TA-dominant production. Therefore, in order to belt, men are not required to change registers. Female singers must have a TA-dominant production with bright speech-like vowels in order to belt. For women with a CT-dominant vocal fold production, developing a belt quality can be challenging. For the classical female singer, the shift to belt may be even more difficult, since it involves a register adjustment and a change from tall, round vowels to bright, narrow vowels and speech-based pronunciation. The most effective approach is to train singers to strengthen the weaker muscle group and to guide the singer in shaping vowels to achieve a more speech-like pronunciation. This is best done with the supervision of a trained voice teacher who can monitor the singer's progress.

Why does belting require special attention?

1. Belting involves high, loud singing for extended periods of time.

2. There is a tendency for singers to add unnecessary pressure to the throat and the surrounding vocal mechanism because of the emotional nature of belted songs. Women especially have a tendency to add more weight to their middle voice than is natural, and must be cautioned against pushing.

3. Singers sometimes ignore basic common sense regarding health care and vocal hygiene. This can lead to serious vocal problems when coupled with strenuous singing and poor technique.

4. Many singers lack a sense of the delicate nature of the vocal mechanism and feel they are invulnerable to vocal problems.

GUIDELINES FOR BELTING

Skillful belting feels:
- easy in your throat
- as if there is very little air escaping
- as if you can move to other pitches easily
- resonant in your mask

Skillful belting sounds:
- full, but not strained or screamed
- clear and ringing
- as if the tone is easy to produce

A skilled belter looks:
- relaxed in the mouth, jaw, and throat
- connected to the emotion of the song
- energetic

Singers who can belt are in demand in contemporary music now more than ever. But if you damage your voice, your singing career may end long before you reach your prime. Singers need to exercise their entire vocal range, even if they never plan to use CT-dominant singing (head voice) in public. Strengthening your CT-dominant vocal fold production for a lighter touch on high notes can also provide a balance for belters that improves the quality of the primary performing register, the belt voice.

Belting is a very vibrant, emotional style of singing, but use caution. If you feel tightness or tickling in your throat when singing, you are probably pushing. While some singers can sing using an easy, unforced belt voice without straining, for others it seems difficult to develop a good sounding belt range without forcing, or sounding as if the tone is swallowed. Forcing your voice not only detracts from the emotion of the music, it can lead to vocal strain and serious vocal problems. *Singers who belt should be sure to obtain the additional training and conditioning needed to prepare their bodies and voices for this dynamic singing style.*

GOOD DICTION MEANS that consonants are articulated, vowels and syllables are enunciated, and words are pronounced in a manner appropriate to the style of music being sung. Proper diction is important for conveying the mood, emotion, and story of a song in any language you use.

FORMAL AND INFORMAL DICTION

In many languages there are different styles of speaking. Language can be formal if one is addressing dignitaries or at a solemn event. Classical music written by English speaking composers, such as Aaron Copland or Benjamin Britten, is pronounced in a more formal, stylized manner. Formal pronunciation, including flipped Rs and big, exploded consonants, can help singers project without electronic amplification in a large room, even over an orchestra.

Contemporary popular music has an informal, colloquial pronunciation similar to spoken English. Informal pronunciation means there are no flipped Rs, and in some styles, singers can change rhythms to follow the natural accents in words and phrases in normal speech. Of course, the contemporary music singer still needs to communicate with an audience. Awareness of the balance between clarity and the subtleties of spoken pronunciation is essential.

MICROPHONES

Most popular singers use a microphone, which affects diction. Their challenge is to enunciate clearly, without sounding overly formal. Also, consonants can produce a popping sound if sung directly into the mic. To eliminate this, singers hold the microphone at an angle to the mouth, lightly articulating Ps and Ts over the top of the mic rather than directly into it (see chapter 10).

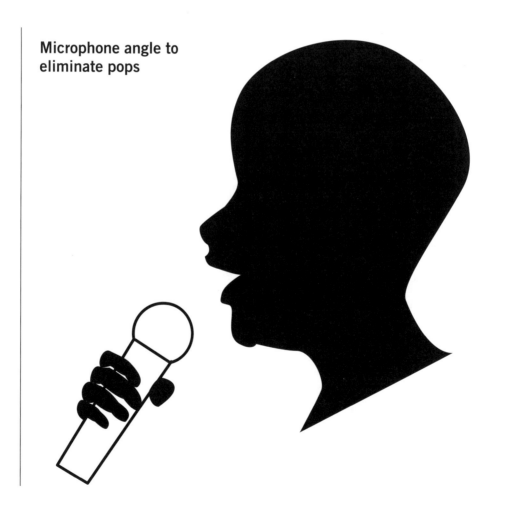

Microphone angle to eliminate pops

SINGING AND NON-SINGING DICTION

Singing with good diction involves a different set of skills than speaking with good diction. First, in singing, vowels are sustained longer than in speech. If a vowel is not clear, sustaining it over a long note makes it even harder to understand.

Second, not all syllables are accented equally. For lyrics to be intelligible, sung words must have the same weak and accented syllables as speech. Your challenge is to avoid emphasizing unaccented syllables, even if the weak syllable is stretched over a long note.

Finally, words are generally sung higher than they are spoken. The slight, natural adjustment to vowel sounds when singing high in your range is called *vowel modification*. This will occur naturally if the tone is resonating efficiently, there is adequate breath support, and the tongue, jaw, and throat are relaxed. Singers should mentally focus on the true vowel, as the mouth and back of the throat open to allow the tone to project freely without sounding pinched (see Vowel Modification on page 48).

Vowels are bright, dark, or neutral in color. These colors occur naturally when vowels are properly pronounced.[2]

FIVE PRIMARY VOWELS

PRIMARY VOWELS

ah	aisle
ay	mate
ee	meet
oh	obey
oo	flute

These five primary vowels are the basis of all English vowels. When you vocalize on these vowels, you can hear your basic vocal sound. Singing scales, arpeggios,

---

2 *See Appendix A for a diction guide containing examples of basic American English vowel sounds, including the five basic vowel sounds with variations, and some foreign language equivalents.*

and other vocal exercises on primary vowels helps you hear your voice clearly and helps you learn to feel consistent resonance over a wide range of notes. This helps you know when your voice needs increased focus or energy. In standard American English, the five primary vowels are found in related forms, some more open or more closed (ee and eh, oh and aw) and combined to make compound vowels (see below).

COMPOUND VOWELS (DIPHTHONGS)

A compound vowel includes more than one vowel sound in a single syllable, as in (my = mah + ee). They are also called diphthongs (double vowels within a single syllable). For most styles of music, the first, or primary, vowel should be sustained on long notes, with the secondary vowel(s) quickly added at the end of the word. In country music, the secondary vowel of a diphthong may be sustained to give the pronunciation a bit of a twang.

DIPHTHONGS

day	*deh ee*
sigh	*sah ee*
now	*na oo*
boy	*bo ee*
no	*no oo*

VOWEL MODIFICATIONS IN YOUR HIGH RANGE

When you sing in the top third of your high range you probably need to modify the vowel you are singing to sound relaxed. The following chart indicates how to modify four of the five primary vowels (ah does not need to be modified).

> **Vowel Modification**
> ee modifies by adding *ih* as in the word "hit"
> ay modifies by adding *eh* as in the word "met"
> oo modifies by adding *oŏ* as in the word "put"
> oh modifies by adding *aw* as in the word "saw"

THREE KINDS OF ATTACKS

Glottal, breathy, and coordinated attacks (see chapter 3) affect diction in different ways.

The harsh *glottal attack* begins tone with a burst of air pressure sounding like a pop. Because this is tiring to the vocal folds and can create excessive choppiness in musical phrases, it should be avoided by linking to the previous word whenever possible.

Try singing, "I am on an airplane," using a single repeated tone, separating each word so you feel small bursts of air at the vocal folds. Now link the words together to create a smooth flow without separation: "Ahee yeah maw na neh ruhplane." The second way of articulating the phrase feels smoother. Skillful word connection, the mark of natural-sounding diction, makes your singing flow. It helps you sing long, connected melodic lines, and helps make your lyrics intelligible. Occasionally, you might find it necessary to use a glottal separation in order to clarify meaning. A gentle glottal attack can be helpful, as in, "Lend me your (/) ear," which otherwise might sound like "Lend me your rear."

Another weak diction habit is a *breathy attack* at the beginning of words, when air escapes before the vocal folds vibrate. This results in an audible H at the beginning of words that start with vowels. If you sing, "I love you," on a single repeated pitch and allow a bit of air to escape before tone begins, it will sound like, "Hi love you." This usually happens unintentionally. You can work to eliminate the H by practicing onset exercises.

Onset Exercises

Practice these slowly, taking care to coordinate the beginning of a tone to avoid a glottal or breathy attack. Repeat the patterns moving up by half steps.

65 *Example 6.1*

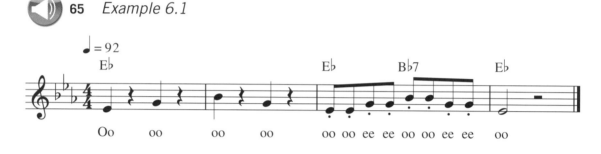

66 *Example 6.2*

The third kind of onset is the coordinated attack, in which breath and voice start together. Not only does this make words beginning with vowels clean and easy to understand, it is not harsh on the vocal folds.

CONSONANTS

Consonants can be voiced or unvoiced. Voiced consonants are sounded using the vibrations of the vocal folds. Unvoiced consonants do not involve vocal fold vibrations (see examples on page 51).

There are several voiced/unvoiced consonant pairs that use the same mouth position. To distinguish voiced and unvoiced consonants, lightly touch the front of your throat at your Adam's apple (larynx). You will feel vibration when you articulate a voiced consonant. Notice the identical positions of the mouth for each pair listed below.

Voiced consonant		Unvoiced consonant	
v	victory, lover	*f*	feeling, life
th	these, wither	*th*	with, thesis, thing
b	biscuit, robber	*p*	pencil, whimper
z	because, does, zoo	*s*	safe, house, whiskers
d	dog, riddle, load	*t*	toe, root, counter

PRONUNCIATION CHECKLIST

1. Rs in words such as free, river, and very are never flipped or trilled as they are in British English or Italian.

2. Rs found at the ends of words or preceding consonants are minimized or eliminated, and the vowel before them is elongated (e.g., charm, harm, word, earth, girl, heart, apart). Soften and *slightly* round the final R in words such as helper, lover, chair, more, and your.

3. Try to link final consonants to the beginning of the next word unless linking compromises the text's meaning. You can also avoid glottal attacks using skillful linking. Try saying, "Emily and Alan argued every other afternoon."

4. Be careful to not reverse R and L. L is articulated with the tip of the tongue lightly touching the back of the top front teeth (see page 52). When articulating the American R, however, the tip of the tongue does not touch the teeth. Instead, the sides of the tongue rise to the teeth as in, "Cry rivers and streams." The American L lightly touches the back of the top front teeth as in, "William, will you lift the yellow lamp?"

5. Many words spelled with the unvoiced S are actually pronounced with a voiced Z, as in wings, charms, arms, and roses. Also, in the word "of," the F is pronounced as a voiced V as in "I think of you. Of course I do."

6. Elongate vowels and quickly articulate consonants at the end of words.

7. The TH consonant combination requires a quick movement of the tongue outward almost beyond the top teeth. It may feel as if you are almost going to stick out your tongue. TH can be voiced, as in "the," or unvoiced as in "with" and "thought." Try saying, "The thoughtless old thing withered away all these months."

8. On diphthongs that are sung over long tones, lengthen the first vowel and gently glide to the second vowel, without emphasizing or lengthening it.

  "Goodbye"   is sung *goodbaaa<u>ee</u>*
  "Yesterday" is sung *yestuhrdaaa<u>ee</u>*

9. Any R that precedes a consonant within a word or in an adjoining word can be minimized and almost eliminated in singing.

  "Heart"   is sung *hahh-rt*
  "Charm"   is sung *chahh-rm*
  "Yesterday"   is sung *ye-stuhr-daa<u>ee</u>*
  "For me"   is sung *fohh-rme*
  "I never saw" is sung *ahee neh-vuhr saw*

10. An R preceding a rest or silence in songs can be slightly muted or completely dropped.

"Scarborough Fair"

Try to incorporate informal pronunciation into this song, including sustaining vowels and minimizing the Rs before consonants.

Example 6.3

Independent tongue movement exercise

Use this exercise to develop facile tongue movement for articulating Ls.

Place one finger on your chin and open your mouth (wide enough to insert two fingers). Extend your tongue to your top teeth, without moving your chin or closing your mouth, and lightly articulate "la, la, la, la, la, la, la, la" on a single pitch. Start slowly, making sure to let the tongue relax down to the bottom of your mouth after each articulated consonant. Go up in pitch by half steps, but stay in the middle of your range and sing lightly. Experiment with vowel sounds like lee or loo.

Example 6.4

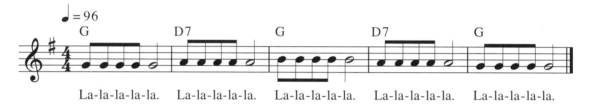

La-la-la-la-la. La-la-la-la-la. La-la-la-la-la. La-la-la-la-la. La-la-la-la-la.

Articulation Exercise

This exercise is helpful in developing skillful linked articulation of W, L, and Y. Repeat the pattern moving up by half steps.

67 *Example 6.5*

Will you, will you, will you, will you   Wil - liam?

Humpty Dumpty Etude

This classic nursery rhyme text is a good articulation exercise. Repeat the pattern moving up by half steps.

 68, 20 HIGH, 44 LOW   *Example 6.6*

Hump - ty Dump - ty sat on a wall,   Hump - ty Dump - ty had a great fall.

All the king's hors-es and all the king's men   could-n't put Hump-ty to-geth-er a-gain.

All the king's hors-es and all the king's men   could-n't put Hump-ty to-geth-er a-gain.

- Practicing
- Maintaining Vocal Health
- Beyond the Basics
- Performing

2

MASTERING THE SKILLS

P RACTICING HELPS you internalize and perfect techniques. You can use practice sessions to learn new tunes, strengthen your voice, extend your breath support, clarify diction, and fine-tune all aspects of your singing.

Practice sessions should be no more than one hour in length. Other instrumentalists, such as guitarists or pianists, seem to be able to practice for hours without problems. However, vocal folds can tire more easily, especially in young or inexperienced singers. Practicing for long periods of time at random, infrequent intervals can reinforce old bad habits and create new problems. Because of this, singers should practice four to six days a week, for thirty to sixty minutes at a time.

If you miss your practice sessions don't become discouraged and quit. Try to get back in the swing of things and pick up where you can. Improve and freshen your practice routine, to keep yourself from becoming bored. When you are training, it is best to be consistent, so don't become discouraged if you have setbacks. Move ahead with renewed commitment.

Plan to rehearse several times well in advance of a performance. This way you can avoid vocal burn out and become completely comfortable with your music before a performance. It will also give you a comfort level that helps you feel more prepared and less anxious about performances. Feeling well prepared goes a long way toward staving off stage fright and nervousness.

PRODUCTIVE PRACTICE

■ Location

If you practice at home, it is important to work where you can relax and not be self-conscious. You need to feel free to make mistakes, and not hold back for fear of disturbing neighbors or family. This might mean scheduling your practice time when others are away. If there is no place at home to practice, inquire at a local school or house of worship to see if there is a room that you could use regularly. Some places charge a small fee to use the facility.

■ Keyboard

Wherever you practice, you will need some kind of keyboard for checking pitches.

■ Mirror

Sometimes singers shy away from the mirror because they are embarrassed to look at themselves, or become distracted and critical of their appearance. Try not to focus on your hair or face, but see your body, posture, and expression in a more detached way, as your instrument. We cannot see the inner workings of our instruments while we are practicing, but we can observe tension in the face, neck, and jaw, which indicates a problem. It is important to use the mirror to help correct awkward or tense looking movements. The muscles of your throat can become tight to compensate for a collapsed chest posture. Align your body in order to allow the muscles of your throat to function freely.

■ Audio Recorder

If you have ever heard a recording of your speaking voice, you probably thought, "That's not how I sound!" This is because we hear our own voices through vibrations inside our heads while others hear our sound conducted through the air. To hear a more realistic (though imperfect) representation of your voice, use a recorder in practice and at your voice lessons. You can learn from hearing your own singing as well as your teacher's comments. Try to listen objectively, and don't be distracted from your goals by being overly critical.

■ Metronome

A metronome will help you establish and maintain tempos when working on songs and keep you from rushing when practicing scales.

ESTABLISH A ROUTINE

An organized practice routine helps you achieve more because you stay mentally focused and waste less time. If you follow this routine daily, you will find that you look forward to your practice time and gain the benefits of daily vocal exercise.

PRACTICE ROUTINE

I. Beginning Warm-up
    a. Physical Stretches (2–3 minutes)
    b. Warm-up Vocalizations (3–5 minutes)
II. Vocal Technique (10–20 minutes)
III. Song Study (15–20 minutes)
IV. Cool Down (2–5 minutes)

I. BEGINNING WARM-UP

You probably wouldn't run a couple of miles before warming up and stretching. In the same way, it is advisable to warm up vocally before working on vocal technique or songs. The equivalent of stretching your legs before you run, vocal warm-ups increase the blood flow to your muscles and gradually release tension to prepare your body for activity. The few minutes of exercises recommended here are intended to prepare your voice for more activity and are generally not enough to completely warm up your instrument. For a more comprehensive warm-up, complete the beginning warm-up and the vocal technique segment of this recommended practice routine.

A. Physical stretches (2–3 minutes)

It is important to begin singing with physical freedom because we sing and perform with our entire bodies, which need to be prepared for activity.

NOTES ON WARM-UPS

1. If you feel pain, stop immediately.
2. Don't hold your breath while stretching.
3. A stretched muscle is in a weakened position, so don't stress it by forcing or bouncing.
4. Read the directions for each exercise thoroughly before attempting it.
5. Choose a few of the following stretches. Do only what feels right and good to you. Listen to your body and use common sense.
6. Modify stretches to suit your needs or physical limitations.

Gentle Head Rolls

Purpose: to stretch the strong muscles of the neck and to release tension.

Let your jaw hang loose and open throughout this stretch. Go at your own pace, circling your head in both directions. If you become dizzy, keep your eyes open.

1. Gently drop your head so your chin is close to your chest, and let the weight of your head stretch the strong muscles of your neck. Do not push your head down—let it hang.

2. Starting from this position, slowly roll your head around until your right ear is close to your right shoulder.

3. Continue rolling your head until you're looking upward, elongating your spine, letting your mouth and jaw hang open, and taking care to avoid dropping your head all the way back, which stresses your neck muscles.

4. Continue the head roll circle until your left ear is near your left shoulder, pausing to stretch your neck.

In a continuous, slow movement, roll your head through each of these positions: chin to chest, ear to shoulder, eyes upward, and ear to shoulder. If you feel tension in a particular spot, pause and let the weight of your head stretch it out before continuing. Complete two or three full rotations and then reverse direction.

Neck Tension Releaser

Purpose: to release tension in neck muscles that may inhibit free laryngeal function in singing.

Your neck muscles are complex and can be susceptible to injury if you force your head into any position. Be gentle with this exercise and use common sense.

1. Lean your right ear to your right shoulder and feel the weight of your head elongate the muscles on the side of your neck.

2. Reach your right arm over the top of your head and rest your right palm on your left ear, simply letting the weight of your arm increase the stretch in your neck muscles. *Do not pull your head.*

3. After you have stretched sufficiently (10–30 seconds), move your arm from your ear and just let your head hang in this position for a few seconds.

4. Next, support your head with your right hand, using it to bring it back to its upright position. To avoid stressing the stretched muscle, don't use your neck muscles alone to pull up your head. Repeat on your left side.

Shoulder Rolls

Purpose: to release tension in the upper back and shoulders.

Many people carry tension in their shoulders. This stretch will help release shoulder tension that might inhibit free vocal production.

Proceed at a slow, relaxed pace, moving from one position to the next without stopping. Focus on using a full range of motion. Remember to breathe normally.

1. Bring both shoulders up to your ears, then roll them back so your shoulder blades almost touch in back.

2. Bring them down to a relaxed position, and then forward to round your upper back.

3. Reverse directions and roll in a continuous motion.

Rib Stretch

Purpose: to stretch and develop awareness of the rib muscles, and improve fullness of breath.

Rib stretches help release tension and prepare your body for the extended breathing used in singing.

1. Stand with your feet about shoulder-width apart.

2. Reach up with your right arm, palm flat to the ceiling, and stretch it upward and over the top of your head while leaning to your left.

3. To increase this stretch, bend your right knee as you stretch your right arm up (your left leg should remain straight). You should feel a good stretch in your right-side rib muscles.

4. Repeat this stretch on your left side.

Full Roll-Down

Purpose: to increase awareness of abdominal and rib expansion during breathing and stretch your back, leg, and postural muscles to release tension.

When you are bent over at the waist, keep your knees loose (not locked) and only bend over as far as it feels comfortable. Do not force your palms to touch the floor.

1. Standing with feet hip-distance apart, slowly drop your chin to your chest. Continue to roll down, leading with your head, proceeding one vertebra at a time until you are bending over at the waist.

2. In this position, take a full breath that expands your belly and ribs (the belly expansion will make you rise from the floor slightly) then exhale. Check the back of your neck to make sure you are not lifting your head, but rather letting the top of your head drop to the floor.

3. Still in this rolled-down position, breathe normally as you slightly bend and straighten your knees a few times, feeling the stretch in the back of your legs.

4. Now shift your weight back slightly, so your hips are over your feet. With slightly bent knees, take one more breath, exhale, and slowly roll up one vertebra at a time, sensing your feet push into the floor. This action will help you use your legs to stand up again, instead of your newly stretched back muscles.

Chewing

Purpose: to induce relaxation in the facial muscles and free your jaw.

Stand or sit in a comfortable, relaxed position and imagine the sensation of your head floating effortlessly toward the ceiling.

1. Pretend you have two large pieces of bubble gum in your mouth, one on each side. Chew with exaggerated movements, with an open mouth, saying "mum-mum-mum."

2. Chew for a few seconds and rest. Do three or four repetitions of these exercises, then rest.

3. Sing or speak a line of text using the chewing action with vigorous movement of the lips, jaw, and cheeks. This exercise can be done in brief intervals throughout the day.[3]

Self-massage

Purpose: to release tension in your neck, facial muscles, and jaw.

You can target your own specific muscle tensions in this self-massage routine.

1. Standing or sitting comfortably and with your head level, massage the back and sides of your neck with the pads of your fingers in a gentle circular motion.

2. Work your fingers up the muscles in front of your ears and along the edge of your jaw.

3. Let your mouth drop open and massage in the soft spot directly under your chin with your thumbs.

4. Gently continue up the back of your neck to your head and place your fingers firmly on your scalp and move your entire scalp around. Imagine air entering between your skull and your scalp.

---

[3] Miller, R. The Structure of Singing: "Froeschel's chewing." (London, Schirmer Books Collier MacMillan Publishing, 1986), pp. 233–255.

5. End your massage by tracing long, firm strokes with your fingers along your eyebrows, one at a time, from the inside corner to the outside corner.

B. Warm-up vocalizations (3–5 minutes)

Sighs, humming, sliding, and lip trills are great for getting the "cobwebs" out and increasing blood flow to your vocal folds. Vocal slides and other nontraditional vocalizations like the ones suggested here allow your voice to function freely and prepare your voice for more vigorous activity.

Slides

Purpose: to begin vocalization exercises; useful especially for singers who are very tense.

During this exercise, check your jaw and neck for tension, and release it as you go. Explore the middle range of your voice, which should flow freely and have a consistent tone quality. Stand in front of a mirror and begin to vocalize by sliding your voice up and down.

1. Start at or slightly above your speaking pitch and gently say, "hoo," letting your voice slide down in pitch in a slow, smooth descent. Imagine that you let the sound fall out of your body without trying to control or manipulate it.

2. Start at a slightly higher pitch and repeat.

3. Continue to a comfortably high level, and then proceed back down again.

Lip Trills

Purpose: to initiate tone production with a steady airflow and relaxed jaw.

Lip trills can be valuable at the start of a warm-up session partly because they sound silly and help free you from inhibitions about singing. Practice to develop evenness in the trilling of your lips and in your tone quality. Don't be discouraged if at first you cannot make your lips bubble consistently. Many singers find that they can vocalize on a lip trill easier than on any other syllable. If this is true for you, take inventory of your vocal production, posture, and the sensations in your throat and neck when trilling. Evaluate how your voice feels and how you might develop the same sense of freedom singing on vowel sounds.

1. First try to make the sound of a motorboat by loosely bubbling your lips without any pitch. Let your jaw hang as if you have no control over the muscles in your mouth and tongue. Start by blowing air over the lips and letting them vibrate.

2. When this becomes consistent, add pitch and slide freely through the middle part of your voice using a descending pattern.

3. If you have tried to make your lips trill without success, place your index fingers gently at each corner of your mouth. If this helps, vocalize lip trills with your fingers in this position. Take care not to slouch if you bring your hands to your mouth. If you still cannot do a lip trill, use the humming exercise instead.

Sliding Warm-up

Combine sliding, which helps induce laryngeal relaxation and lip trills, to maintain a consistent airflow, for an effective beginning warm-up. Repeat the pattern moving up by half steps.

69
3 BEGINNING WARM-UP *Example 7.1*

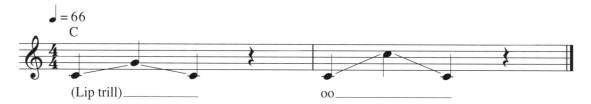

Humming

Purpose: to initiate tone production while increasing your awareness of forward resonance.

Light humming can be an ideal beginning vocalization because the buzzing sensation in your lips, mouth, and nose helps ensure correct natural tone placement.

1. Take a relaxed breath and lightly hum with your lips barely touching. The inside edges of your lips should buzz with vibrations.

2. As you continue to vocalize, first with descending slides, then with descending fifths pitched at the keyboard, try to feel the vibrations in your "mask."

Descending Hum/Slides

 70 *Example 7.2*

II. VOCAL TECHNIQUE (10–20 MINUTES)

This part of practicing will complete your warming up and help you work out vocally. During technique work, identify what you need to improve in your singing (increasing range, agility, breath control, improving tone quality). Regular vocal technique work will help keep your voice in shape, ready for the demands of singing. The purpose of technical work is to develop new skills and reinforce muscle memory. In singing, we learn by intellectually understanding concepts and by training muscles. It is both an intellectual and a physical process.

If you have skipped the beginning warm-up, I recommend that you back up and complete 2–3 minutes of light vocalizing first. Though many singers start practice by vocalizing scales, preceding vocal technique work with a beginning warm-up that includes physical stretches and easy vocalizing on a descending slide pattern is much more sensible. If you are working on vocal flexibility and agility, for example, you may find that your voice feels sluggish and resistant to quick, light movements, if you have not warmed up. If you complete the recommended beginning warm-up, you can work more directly toward free, agile production and avoid the frustration of trying to sing before your voice is free and your body is relaxed.

Identify your goals for your vocal technique practice. Have a purpose for every exercise or scale you sing. You can adapt exercises you know to suit your needs or make up your own exercises. Repeat the patterns moving up by half steps.

Major/Minor Triplet for Flexibility

71, 9 HIGH, 33 LOW   *Example 7.3*

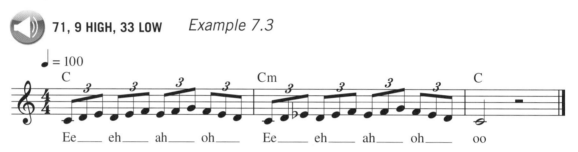

Extended Five-Note Pattern for Flexibility and Breath

72, 10 HIGH, 34 LOW   *Example 7.4*

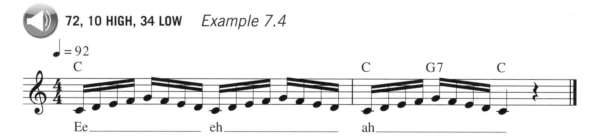

Two Fives and a Nine for Flexibility, Range, and Breath

73   *Example 7.5*

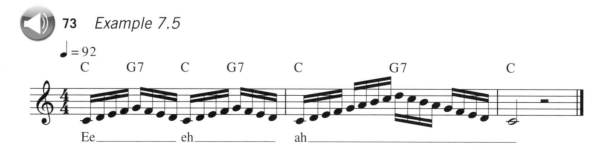

Legato Flexibility Exercise

 74, 21 HIGH, 45 LOW   *Example 7.6*

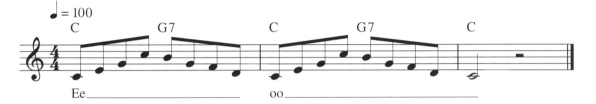

Long Tones for Vowel Equalization and Breath Extension

 75, 16 HIGH, 40 LOW   *Example 7.7*

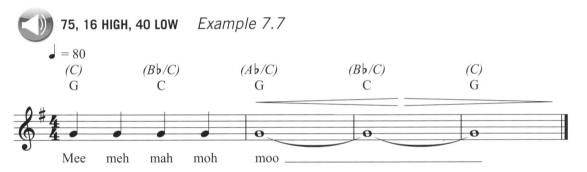

Octave Arpeggio for Range Extension and Flexibility

 76, 13 HIGH, 37 LOW   *Example 7.8*

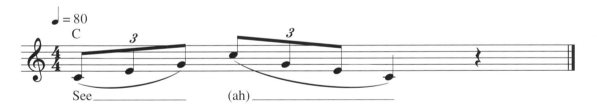

III. SONG STUDY (15–20 MINUTES)

It takes more flexibility to sing words and melody together, so after you have warmed up and worked out, your voice should be ready for the more demanding task of singing songs. This part of your practice routine is set aside to perfect notes and rhythms, study lyrics, add stylistic interpretation and combine all these details into a technical and musical whole.

Seven steps to learning a new song

1. Rhythm

It is important to learn the notes and rhythms of your songs first. Take the time to read through the song rhythmically, and clap, or say "tah," on the written rhythms. Use a metronome to maintain a steady beat, and don't skip this step just because you already know the song from a recording. Recording artists take liberties with written notes and rhythms. You need to know the original written notes and rhythms to see what the composer intended—then you can make it your own interpretation. In some styles of music you can take a great deal of liberty with the rhythms, and in other styles it is not appropriate.

2. Melody

After learning the rhythms, plunk out the melody on a keyboard. Learn the shape of the tune and review any tricky intervals, without worrying about keeping a strict rhythm. How does the melody lie in your voice? You should be able to sing through the song without straining.

If the song feels too high or too low, experiment, singing it in different keys. Once you have decided on a key, you need written music or a lead sheet in that key. Do not ask an accompanist to transpose on sight during an audition or performance. Computer programs can transpose tunes and produce charts that are easy to read. Band-in-a-Box, for example, includes the accompaniment for many tunes and allows you to transpose them easily. Finale and Sibelius require more skill, but can produce better, more sophisticated charts.

Jazz standards and pop tunes are often transposed into a key that suits the singer's voice. Some musical theater pieces, such as songs by Cole Porter, have become jazz standards and also can be transposed. Opera arias, however, are usually performed in the key in which they were written. The same goes for classic musical theater repertoire (e.g., *Oklahoma, Carousel, The King and I*) and other music of this genre, which is generally intended for specific voice types.

3. Rhythm and melody without lyrics

Stand up, away from the piano or keyboard, and sing your song in rhythm on a favorable vowel sound, but without the lyrics. Make the melody flow from note to note, observe dynamic markings, and check tricky rhythms and intervals. Plan where you will breathe, and work out your phrasing by marking (') in your music. This basic groundwork will save you time in the long run. If you've planned your phrasing well, you won't get stuck having to breathe in the middle of a word or run out of air at the end of phrases.

4. Add basic accompaniment

Sing the melody in rhythm on a favorable vowel with the accompaniment or basic chord changes—don't skip this step. Never take a song into an audition or performance situation without first working with the accompaniment. It can change your entire concept of the melody and throw you off balance in the pressure of a performance situation. If you are working from a lead sheet, there are many ways a song can be harmonized or played with a different rhythmic feel. It depends on your accompanist and how well you describe the rhythmic feel and tempo you want.

5. Study the lyrics

Look up words you don't understand, and look for underlying meaning in the text. Can you relate to it enough to give a good interpretation? You don't need to have lived the story of a song to sing it, but you should be able to empathize enough with the lyrics to give a meaningful interpretation. Think of yourself as an actor interpreting dramatic text for an audience.

6. Listen to recordings

Listen to recordings by other artists and make observations that help you define your concept of a song. Constantly imitating the sound of other singers is not vocally healthy. However, you can learn a great deal from recordings by observing the phrasing, tempo, rhythmic feel, and interpretation. How does the singer interpret the melody, rhythm, and harmony? Is the key of the song higher or lower than the key you are singing? Notice the singer's voice quality. Do you like it? Is the rhythmic feel or groove in the accompaniment what you imagined it would be like? How is it different from the printed music? What is the style of the song (ballad, up-tempo, rock, jazz, Latin, etc.)? Answering these questions when you listen will help you fine-tune your concept of a song.

7. Interpret the song

Interpreting means adding your own personal expression to a song. It can be in the way you deliver the lyrics, or if stylistically appropriate, changes to the melody or rhythm. It also includes changes from specified dynamics, a different harmonization, addition or subtraction of vibrato in your voice, and experimenting with different vocal colors. Interpretation should come after you do the basic groundwork to learn a piece.

The best way to begin is to study the text. If you address the lyrics, the rest will come with practice and experience. Understand what you are singing and try to express the feelings and emotions of the lyrics to your audience. If you watch yourself in a mirror, you will see that subtle expression in your eyes can enhance your communication of a song. Singers can also learn to interpret by studying standard songs and transcribing the actual melodies sung by great singers. Studying what great singers do with a song can spark your own ideas.

IV. COOL DOWN (2–5 MINUTES)

It is as important to cool down vocally after practice as it is to cool down after a physical workout. The purpose is to bring your vocal folds back to a less active state so your speaking voice doesn't feel unstable. By easing the transition of your vocal mechanism from one activity to another, there is less shock to your voice. It is especially important to cool down if you are going out into cold weather, or if you have been singing high notes for a while.

To cool down, repeat the body and voice work of the beginning warm-up from the first part of your practice session. Are your shoulders or other parts of your body sore after practice? Stretch out physically, targeting the tension spots in your body. Lighter stretches can be combined with light humming or sighs, and you should also repeat some of the less intense technical exercises.

Mental practicing

Mental practicing is rehearsing without using your voice. It can be used when you are vocally tired, ill, or when you are healthy but are not mentally focused enough on the tasks at hand. Mental practice not only rests your voice, but also can bring mental alertness back to a practice session and be an effective method of problem solving. It can also be used to take a break from regular vocal practice to conserve your voice.

If you mentally practice a song with intensity, you can learn without actually singing. Athletes know that mental practicing can help solve problems as well as fine-tune performance. As we sit in an armchair mentally practicing, we actually produce muscle contractions (so small they cannot be felt) that are similar to the ones we produce when we perform. Try this guided imagery exercise to improve your mental focus.

Guided imagery exercise

Relax in a comfortable chair and notice your breathing. It should be deep and relaxed. Imagine yourself in the place where you usually practice or perform. Imagine how quiet and peaceful the surroundings are. Now imagine the details: the floor, the height of the ceiling, the smell of the room, the temperature, the sound and feel of the place. Mentally go to the place in this room where you sing. Notice how your muscles feel as you prepare to sing. Take inventory of your body position in this imagined space, and feel the anticipation of the performance. Imagine yourself taking a deep breath and beginning your song, singing through each phrase flawlessly. In your imagery, you will always breathe in the right spots and sing the way you want. Proceed through your performance phrase by phrase, not skipping, but singing the song all the way through in your mind. Sing through the performance feeling you have done your best.

Repeat this exercise, emphasizing your awareness of sound, and feel. It is important to see yourself succeed. Imagine your sense of pride in your accomplishment at the end of your mental practice. Sense the feel, sounds, and energy of a live audience. Imagine a positive audience reaction and your feeling of accomplishment.

Strong emotions are involved in the mental practice of correct vocal skills. During your guided imagery, if negative thoughts or mistakes creep into your thinking, stop the imagery, rewind it like a videotape in your mind, and proceed forward again in slow motion, frame by frame, seeing yourself execute the trouble spots easily, without any catches. Work through any negative thoughts and turn them into positive images.

Breathing for relaxation

Breath is essential to making sound for singing. Concentrating on deep breathing before practice and performance will help relax your muscles and focus your mind. With a focused mind and relaxed body, you will be ready for singing. If you don't take the time to relax, you will find singing is much harder work. You may be fighting with residual tension and negative thoughts that prevent efficient muscle coordination.

Take a deep breath, imagining you fill up the bottom of your lungs first. Let your abdomen relax and ribs open. Breathe in through your nose and mouth. Your throat should feel relaxed. Your diaphragm will stretch downward and your abdomen should relax outward allowing your lungs to expand. Let your ribs relax and exhale all of your air. Draw your abdominal muscles in to completely empty your lungs. Remember to inhale and think of relaxation, exhale and release any tension. Repeat this exercise several times over the course of the day to release tension and invigorate your body and mind. This exercise is specifically for releasing tension and improving mental focus. It is similar to the breath action used in singing, but in relaxation exercises, your rib muscles don't resist the action of your diaphragm during exhalation.

I F SINGERS WERE to sing only when they feel completely healthy and stress free, many of us would never be able to make a living performing. That is why it is important to prevent problems by knowing yourself, your voice, your limits, and how to take care of yourself. The state of your voice reflects the state of your overall health. Therefore, it is key that you take care of your whole self in order to experience vocal benefits.

VOCAL HEALTH—FACTS[4]

1. Good vocal quality and endurance are extremely important for personal and professional communication as well as singing.

2. Voice disorders ranging from hoarseness to laryngitis are common. The cause can originate from serious vocal abuse or other physical problems, such as allergies.

[4] From "Vocal Health," by Robert Thayer Staloff, M.D., D.M.A., www.phillyent.com/patienteducation/articles.php.

3. Changes in voice quality or endurance can indicate the presence of serious problems or illness. Consequently, all voice disorders warrant professional evaluation.

4. Most voice problems can be corrected.

5. Voice disorders may lead to permanent voice impairment. Accurate diagnosis and treatment can help the singer avoid long-term problems.

6. The standard of voice care has improved dramatically in the past 30 years. With this progress in treatment and care, singers shouldn't be afraid to go to the laryngologist.

VOCAL HEALTH GUIDELINES

Hydration

One of the easiest ways we can positively affect our health is to maintain adequate hydration. If your body is well hydrated, then your larynx will benefit.

One of the most common voice problems is dry vocal folds. If your body does not have enough fluids, then your vocal folds become dry and your voice will not function properly.

Speaking and singing with dry vocal folds often results in vocal problems such as voice breaks, excessive throat clearing (which further irritates your vocal folds), loss of volume control or range, vocal fatigue, and voice loss.

A person who doesn't make a lot of demands on their voice might not notice the symptoms of dry vocal folds. Most professional voice users, including doctors, ministers, lawyers, and teachers know how a dry, tired voice can impact daily work.

Your vocal folds require a thin layer of mucus to keep them vibrating properly. If your vocal folds are not well lubricated, then voice use generates a lot of friction that can tire out your voice. Just as a car engine needs oil to keep it running smoothly, your vocal folds need to be lubricated to function smoothly. Your vocal folds become lubricated when your entire body is well hydrated. The best lubrication can be achieved by drinking plenty of water well in advance of heavy voice use. This gives your body time to absorb the water and distribute the fluids to all the tissues of your body, including your larynx. A good rule of thumb (if you have normal kidney and heart function) is to drink at least two quarts of water daily.

Some singers follow this rule: "Pee pale, sing clear." This means that if your urine is light colored or almost clear, it can indicate that your body is well hydrated. Certain medications and vitamin supplements can affect the color of urine, so speak to your doctor if you have questions about this.

You can hydrate your vocal folds from the inside out by drinking water, as mentioned above, and topically by inhaling steam. There are gadgets made to sit on a tabletop that create a controlled amount of steam that you can inhale through your nose and mouth via a plastic mask, or you can stand over a pot of simmering water. These tools are useful if you have a cold and want to clear some of the thick mucus secretions from your nasal passages and throat. They also are valuable if you are traveling to perform. But, for most singers, they are not necessary to use daily, unless you live in a particularly dry environment.

Even if you drink enough water each day, there are several other causes of a dry voice.

Caffeine and Alcohol

Caffeine and alcohol dehydrate your system and deplete your vocal folds of needed lubrication. Caffeinated drinks include coffee, tea, some fortified vitamin waters (usually identified as "energy drinks"), and soft drinks. Wine, beer, and hard liquor are all drying to the system as well. Small amounts of these beverages can be tolerated, but should be counterbalanced by drinking more water to compensate for the diuretic effect of caffeine and alcohol, especially if you are making singing and speaking demands on your voice.

Other non-caffeinated beverages such as juice and decaffeinated coffee/tea will hydrate your body too, but water is the best choice for pure hydration with no additives—acids that can irritate, or ingredients that can coat your throat, such as sugar.

Environment

Another factor that can affect hydration is a dry air environment. Home heating season can be very drying to our bodies. The cause can be gas, oil, or electric furnaces, or in the summer, air conditioners, as well as climates with a low amount of moisture in the air. Using a humidifier at night can help compensate for the dryness in the air.

Another particularly dry environment is on an airplane (See Traveling, p. 85).

Medications

Some medications can contribute to dry voice as well. Antihistamines and cold medicines control the watery secretions of colds and allergies, but also can dry you out excessively. Inhalers used for asthma can dry and irritate your throat as well, but are a necessary medication for some people. Some antidepressants can cause dryness as well. The benefits can outweigh the side effects, and you should never stop taking a prescription medication without consulting your doctor. Many times, medication-induced dryness can be remedied by increasing water intake.

If singing hurts, don't sing.

As simple as this sounds many singers get caught up in the moment and don't listen to their bodies when they are tired and should rest vocally. Disregard for your own vocal health, combined with pressure from a music director or bandleader to rehearse songs repeatedly, can tire or strain your voice.

Pain in your larynx can be a sign of a problem. Singers experiencing pain, huskiness, or hoarseness and loss of high range should see a throat specialist (laryngologist) experienced in working with singers. Performing arts venues, music colleges, conservatories, and other singers can usually refer you to such a doctor.

Often, general "ear, nose, and throat" doctors (otolaryngologists) do not have the specialized expertise in performing-arts medicine to optimally help vocalists.

Singers should watch for signs of vocal fold swelling, characterized by slight hoarseness or raspiness, a speaking voice that feels huskier than normal, and a vocal quality that sounds coarse and less than clean. Frequently, there is a loss of high range, the upper passaggio (chapter 5) feels unstable, and you need more breath support than normal because of inefficient vocal fold vibrations due to swelling. A virus can cause this type of problem, as can overuse of your voice.

If you have what seems to be more than a simple cold, consult a qualified specialist for advice and treatment.

Sometimes, when singers suspect a problem beyond a cold, they delay going to a doctor because they don't want a serious vocal problem to be confirmed. Don't delay! Go to a laryngologist who works with singers. A skilled specialist will be more sensitive to your personal feelings about your singing. They can offer advice regarding any upcoming singing engagements.

Singing over a cold.

There are times when you can sing with a cold and times when you should absolutely rest your voice. When an occasional cold comes on, you can rely on breath support and body awareness to get through rehearsals and concerts without exacerbating fatigue or doing permanent damage.

You can usually sing over a cold if you have nasal congestion but no throat symptoms. You might have a bit of nasality to your tone, but in general, congestion can be sung over (or through). The first line of treatment for your singing voice is moisture. Drink a lot of water to keep your vocal tract mucus thin. Inhaling steam topically moisturizes the vocal folds. Cough drops can keep you from coughing to the point of hoarseness, but the sugar and menthol in them can dry you out. Caffeine, alcohol, and smoking should be avoided because these are all drying to your voice and body. Herbal teas (caffeine-free) can be soothing and add moisture back to your system as well.

Sprays that numb throat pain are usually not recommended for singers. Throat pain indicates that you should not be singing. Singing while you are numbing your throat pain with sprays, aspirin, ibuprofen, acetaminophen, or anything else, can be a recipe for problems. Consult your doctor for advice about the use of any medication.

When you have a cold, focus on your breath support, and pay close attention to your voice for any signs of fatigue.

Choose your repertoire carefully, and avoid music that is unusually taxing in range or intensity.

If you need to change the key of a song, do it. It is not an artistic compromise to transpose pop songs into a comfortable range. Many contemporary singers are men with unusually high ranges, such as Stevie Wonder and Sting, or women with high belt voices, such as Whitney Houston and Celine Dion. Work to extend your range with scale patterns and exercises. But remember that some songs may not be right for your voice, no matter how much you like them.

Develop your own unique voice.

You should listen to great singers, study them, transcribe and sing great solos, listen to phrasing, and try to figure out what makes these singers unique. But remember that it is not vocally healthy to continually imitate others to the exclusion of developing your own voice. Voices often don't fully mature until singers are in their mid-twenties or even into their thirties, so be patient and don't force your voice.

Pay attention to the way you speak.

Over the course of a day, most of us speak far more than we sing, and as singers, we need to be aware of how we use our voices in speech. Beyond being a means of communication, your voice is a vital part of your personality and psyche, and you should treat it with care.

Singers can be gregarious, outgoing, and emotional people. Because your instrument produces both your speaking and singing voice, it follows that your singing can be negatively affected by poor speaking habits. To prevent this, employ touch-distance talking.[5] Only speak to those who are within an arm's length, or touching distance, away. This will help you control the urge to shout and prevent unnecessary strain on your voice.

In some cultures, people tend to speak in lower pitched, less resonant voices. While this characterization of a low or husky voice especially affects the way women speak, many men also speak in a lower voice than is comfortable in order to command respect or convey a businesslike seriousness. This can be detrimental to singing, dragging down your voice and making your muscles work harder than necessary to produce sound.

Singers who habitually speak too low can adversely affect their tone production. The tendency to speak too low can make a singer timid about singing high notes. You can benefit from observing yourself and your speech habits for patterns that may be wearing to your voice.

Check where you tend to pitch your voice by speaking a phrase and finding its approximate pitch on the piano. Try to elongate a syllable and find a range where your speaking voice lies. If you speak much lower than you sing, imagine that you are elevating the focus of your speaking voice (placement, chapter 5) from chest resonance to more nasal resonance rather than raising your pitch. You may find that this results in a slight pitch change, but that it feels and sounds more natural than actually trying to speak at a higher pitch. Make sure you are phonating clearly. In addition, support your speaking voice as if you were singing, using a steady flow of breath.

---

[5] *Burk, K. "Reducing Vocal Abuse: 'I've Got to Be Me.'" Language, Speech and Hearing Services in Schools, vol. 22 (Rockville, MD: American Speech-Language-Hearing Association), pp. 173–178.*

To avoid problems and to keep your voice healthy, it is important to:

- speak with ease (avoid talking over a background of noise, and avoid a compressed or forced sound)

- speak at an appropriate pitch range

- use appropriate amplification when speaking to a large audience or in a room with poor acoustics

- speak with coordinated onset of tone (rather than hard glottal attacks)

- use adequate breath support

Whispering is tiring to your vocal folds, so don't make the mistake of thinking it conserves your voice. You can actually strain your voice by whispering when you should be resting vocally.

Avoid prolonged talking around noise, dust, and smoke.
Performing

Performing environments such as theaters, clubs, and bars are often dusty, smoky, and noisy—all things to be avoided by singers. While this is often out of your control, you can do some things to help prevent vocal burnout.

1. Avoid smoky areas.

Do your best to avoid smoke filled rooms and don't hang around smoky areas on your breaks.

2. Keep quiet on breaks.

Talking over background music and other noise makes you talk louder than normal and can lead to vocal strain.

3. Avoid alcohol and caffeine while performing.

Your vocal folds should be well lubricated for your voice to function best. Alcohol and caffeine dry your body and vocal mechanism, so it is best to avoid them when you are performing. Alcohol can also limit your judgment about how loud you are singing, impair your ability to sing in tune, and lead to unnecessary strain. Drinks containing alcohol and caffeine can also lead to reflux laryngitis (see page 87).

Traveling

In cars, airplanes, trains, and other vehicles, background noise forces you to speak louder than normal, which can be detrimental to your voice.

1. Airplanes

The air on planes is typically very dry and recycled throughout the plane—conditions that dehydrate the vocal mechanism and body. Responding to a talkative seatmate on a long flight can wear out your voice. Drinking alcohol can compound this wear and tear.

Before traveling, prepare your body by super-hydrating, drinking eight to ten glasses of water a day for several days beforehand.

2. Cars

It is one thing to sing along to the radio as you drive in a car, and quite another to practice there. Background noise makes you have to sing louder to hear yourself. Your posture is compromised by the car seat, so you are not as likely to support your voice adequately. It is more productive to practice in a place where you can really hear yourself and concentrate on what you are doing.

Avoid throat clearing.

Throat clearing is hard to avoid when you have a stubborn spot of thick mucus rattling around and you're trying to sing. But when you clear your throat, you not only remove the bothersome mucus, you can irritate the leading edges of your vocal folds. This makes your body produce more mucus to protect them. It becomes a circular problem, so coughing and throat clearing should be avoided. When practicing, try to sing the mucus off. If you must clear your throat, do it gently, and avoid habitual throat clearing.

If you have severe coughing spasms caused by bronchial irritation, see a doctor. You might benefit from medication that controls coughing, thereby minimizing irritation to your vocal folds. A doctor's treatment may also involve antibiotics, reflux treatment, or mucus-thinning medications, such as guaifenesin. Be aware that many over-the-counter decongestants have the tendency to dry out your vocal folds.

Develop good rehearsal habits.

Warming up before rehearsals will help you avoid straining your voice. During a long rehearsal, be sure to take breaks, drink plenty of water, use a well-positioned monitor that lets you hear yourself sing with an amplified band, and conserve your voice by marking (see page 93) when necessary. Do not schedule a long rehearsal the evening before or the day of a performance; you could overtire your voice.

Stay physically fit.

Your body is your instrument. Whatever you do to improve the health of your body and mind eventually shows up in your voice as increased vitality and energy. Singing is physically demanding, and maintaining good health is essential to career success. Physical exercise can help you stay physically and mentally alert, as well as have more energy.

Eat well-balanced meals.

Eat lightly and well in advance of a performance. Large amounts of food and liquid take up space in your body and may interfere with breath management. Milk products can cause excessive mucus production and should be avoided before singing, if it affects you adversely.

Reflux

In a reflux patient, the larynx looks red and swollen under the vocal folds and where the vocal folds open and close at the back of the larynx. The vocal folds sometimes don't close all the way because of the swelling, and there is a husky quality to the voice. Hoarseness, vocal fatigue, a sensation of a lump in the throat, and constant throat clearing are all signs of reflux.

Causes of Reflux

The term *reflux* means a backward flow of stomach acid into the throat. Some people have an abnormal amount of reflux of stomach acid. Age, excess body weight, and pregnancy can aggravate reflux as well.

When we eat, the food travels down to the stomach through the esophagus. In the stomach, acid and enzymes digest food. There are two valves that keep the contents of the stomach from backing up into the esophagus. One valve is above the stomach, and one is at the top of the throat. If the acid travels up past the first valve, it is called GERD or Gastroesophageal Reflux Disease. If the acid makes it into the back of the throat past the second valve, it is called LPRD or Laryngopharyngeal Reflux Disease.

Dr. Steven Zeitels, director of the Division of Laryngology at the Massachusetts Eye and Ear Infirmary in Boston, notes that most individuals with laryngeal reflux do not have heartburn, as is commonly thought. Reflux increases the mucus production often associated with throat clearing, produces an ill-defined feeling of fullness in the throat, and can cause hoarseness, chronic coughing, and difficulty in swallowing. Consuming soda, citrus, spicy foods, caffeine, and alcohol can precipitate and aggravate reflux. Singers should consult with a laryngologist if this is suspected to be a problem.

Treatment of Reflux

There are two ways to help control reflux: behavioral and medicinal.

Controlling Your Reflux by Changing Your Behaviors

Elevate the Head of Your Bed: If you tend to reflux mostly at night, you can raise the head of your bed 4 to 6 inches with bricks, wood blocks, or books so you're sleeping at about a 10 degree slant. This method uses gravity to help keep the contents of your stomach in your stomach.

Control Stress: If you take significant steps to reduce stress, reflux can be managed better. Even moderate stress can dramatically increase the amount of reflux. Some activities that can help include walking, listening to music, running, biking, reading, or meditation.

Avoid Certain Foods: Pay attention to how your system reacts to various foods. Each person will discover which foods cause an increase in reflux. Some of the foods known to increase stomach acid production are:

1. Spicy foods
2. Chocolate
3. Coffee
4. Fatty foods
5. Peppermint
6. Red wine
7. Citrus fruit and juices
8. Tomato products

Mealtime: Eat moderate amounts of food and try not to overindulge. Avoid bedtime snacking, and try to eat your last meal of the day several hours before bedtime. Avoid eating heavily before exercise as well.

Body Weight: Try to maintain a healthy body weight. Being significantly overweight has been shown to increase the amount of reflux.

Avoid Tight Clothing: Tight belts and other restrictive clothing can force the contents of your stomach back up into your esophagus, especially when you bend over or sit.

Don't Smoke; Avoid Smoky Places: Smoking has been shown to increase the severity of reflux. If you smoke, try to stop for the health of your instrument. Inhaling hot chemicals over your delicate vocal folds, and exacerbating the flow of stomach acid in your throat, is going to make your throat irritated and wear away the healthy mucosal lining of your throat. Marijuana smoke is very unhealthy for your voice as well. The increased stomach acid and hot chemicals drawn in through your mouth, throat, vocal folds, and lungs can predispose you to cancer.

Special considerations for singers

According to Robert Sataloff, M.D., in his book, *Professional Voice: The Science and Art of Clinical Care* (Plural Publishing, 3rd edition, 2005), there are several reasons why singers are especially prone to reflux. He states that the energetic use of the abdominal muscles in singing "support" can induce reflux by pushing the stomach up.

Also, the eating habits performers develop can aggravate reflux. When singers don't eat before a performance (due to habit or nervousness) and wait until afterward when it is late, and then go to sleep on a full stomach, reflux problems can flair up. Lying down with a full stomach encourages the food and stomach acid to merge back into the esophagus. The ideal situation for performers would be instead to eat a small meal several hours well in advance of a performance. Eating late at night should be avoided.

Controlling Your Reflux via Medicine

Sometimes, monitoring stress, foods, body weight, and clothing is not enough. In the event that another course of treatment is needed, there are several over-the-counter remedies available. If you think you have reflux-related voice problems, consult your doctor, who can help determine an appropriate treatment plan for you.

Eating disorders such as bulimia and anorexia plague many people, and can ruin your voice and health. In a music career, appearance can be considered very important and singers sometimes take desperate measures to be thin. Laxative abuse, bingeing and purging, starving, and abusing weight-loss drugs can sap your vitality and strength. Repeated vomiting erodes the lining of your throat and mouth and irritates your throat. Because these urges can become uncontrollable and seriously affect your health, if you think you have an eating disorder, get professional help.

Get plenty of rest.

Everyone has different needs for sleep. Know how much sleep you need to function best and maintain a regular sleep schedule as much as you can. Rest your voice whenever possible. Schedule time to unwind during your day. This will help you have renewed energy when you need to sing. Don't wait until you burn out before you schedule down-time away from stressful activities.

If you sing with an amplified band, always use a microphone.

Singers who cannot hear themselves tend to compensate by over-singing. This is a sure way to wear out your voice. Use a microphone when singing with an amplified band. Position yourself so you can hear your voice from an amp or monitor.

Keep your microphone in a separate bag that's easy to locate in your living space. This will be your gig bag, ready to go at a moment's notice. All you have to do is grab it and go. In addition to your microphone, it should contain a mic cord and XLR-to-1/4 inch transformer for connecting to a guitar or keyboard amp. Find out about the sound system, monitor, and other equipment in the performance space so you will know what to bring.

Medications can affect your voice.

Medications can have side effects that are drying, or make you cough, or affect your platelet function so your vocal folds might be prone to a hemorrhage if you aren't careful about voice use.

Only a trained doctor or voice specialist can evaluate your need for medications. Ask your doctor about prescription and nonprescription medications and their effects on your voice.

Here is a list of frequently prescribed medications that can affect your voice. The list was compiled in 1999 by pharmacists and includes two hundred of the most frequently prescribed medications. www.ncvs.org/e-learning/rx2.html

Here is another resource listing medications including over-the-counter medications, that can affect your voice. www.entnet.org/healthinformation/medsvoice.cfm

Do not smoke.

Any singer who is serious about having a career in music should not smoke.

Smoking has long been known to cause emphysema and cancer of the mouth and vocal tract. It irritates vocal tract membranes and your vocal folds. When these membranes are dry and irritated from the chemicals in smoke, your body tries to compensate with secretions. These make you need to clear your throat, which causes further irritation.

Take care of yourself.

Many singers complain of being sick with various colds and illnesses all year long. But if they examine their daily voice use, practice habits, and vocal hygiene, the most basic elements of maintaining good health are being slighted or ignored.

TIPS FOR HEALTHY LIVING

- Eat a variety of healthful foods including whole grains, fruits, and vegetables.
- Get enough sleep at regular hours.
- Stick to a moderate exercise routine.
- Wash your hands with soap and warm water frequently.
- Drink six to eight 8 oz. glasses of water each day.

You only have one voice.

An excellent singer possesses a combination of healthy technique along with emotion and artistry. If a singer has the heart or emotion but does not have healthy technique, then a potential lifetime of voice use will be shortened. Each person has his/her own limit of tolerance for being able to use behaviors that compensate for inadequate technique. For example, if you repeatedly lift heavy objects using your back muscles instead of your legs, then your back will eventually give out. In the same way, if you sing with a manipulated vocal system then sooner or later there will be a technical breakdown because your vocal system will have reached its tolerance limit. Problems typically arise due to a body change (such as pregnancy) or from long-term improper vocal technique.

There is a wide range of ways we can use our voices professionally as singers. Those of us who are singers are also often teachers, choral directors, or worship leaders. There are also many full- and part-time professional singers in a wide range of genres holding down other jobs too. No matter what you do as a professional voice user, your voice requires peak performance for career longevity.

Singing problems may be due to long-term problems with vocal technique, or from overcompensating when sick, causing excess tension. This excess tension or imbalance in vocal technique can put a lot of drag on the delicately balanced vocal mechanism, causing us to compensate by pushing. Signs of vocal problems include:

- vocal fatigue

- tightness in the throat

- change in voice quality

- pain or soreness in muscles of the throat and neck

- hoarseness/breathiness

- voice cuts out

- loss of high range

- stressed or pushed sound

Caring for your singing voice includes caring for your overall health, because your body is your instrument. Your voice quality and resilience reflect the state of your overall health. Remember that you must treat your speaking voice with care because good habits in speaking will influence your singing as well.

Considerations in maintaining your singing voice:

- Warm up before you sing full voice.

- Keep your voice in shape with regular practice.

- Don't over sing during rehearsals. Learn to "mark."

- Be sure you can hear yourself by singing in a room with some natural echo or good acoustics, or by using adequate amplification when necessary.

- Stay well hydrated.

- Maintain a regular sleep schedule.

- Check with your doctor if you have any questions or if you notice changes in your voice.

MARKING FOR VOICE CONSERVATION

Marking is a way of singing that helps you save your voice during rehearsals. To mark a melody, sing just the first few notes of a phrase, and mentally sing the other notes. Raise the lowest and lower the highest notes in your song by an octave (octave displacement) to avoid the extremes of your range. Men can use falsetto to approach high notes. All singing should be light when you are marking.

Marking saves your voice by minimizing its use. It should be used when you are not feeling well, or during rehearsals scheduled just before a performance. Too much practicing before a performance can take the freshness out of your voice. In theater music, singers mark during lighting and technical rehearsals, when it is not important for them to sing at full volume.

Singers often have strong emotions when performing and become carried away by the moment, losing self-control and singing full voice when they should be resting, so listen to your body.

The marking examples are intended to give singers an idea of how to conserve their voices. Notice how the examples eliminate high notes, condensing the melody to a smaller range and omitting every other phrase.

The altered melodies suggested for marking might be too low for tenors and high sopranos. Adjust markings and song keys to suit your voice. There are no set rules. Marking is successful if you benefit from rehearsal while conserving your voice.

TIPS FOR MARKING

What to do when marking

1. Warm up lightly first.
2. Maintain energetic breath support.
3. Sing only the first few words of a phrase, singing the rest mentally.
4. Displace notes at the high and low extremes of your range by an octave to avoid straining. Plan this in advance.
5. Men can sing high notes in falsetto when marking.
6. Always sing lightly when marking.

What to avoid when marking

1. Don't sing everything down an octave.
2. Don't whisper or withhold breath support.
3. Don't lose concentration.
4. Don't succumb to pressure from peers or directors and sing full voice against the advice of your doctor.
5. Don't mark all of the time. You should sing a concert, recital, or other long performance using your full voice several times over a period of several weeks

or longer to make sure you are familiar with phrasing and breath pacing, and to help you develop stamina.

Marking example: "Shenandoah"

The melody of "Shenandoah" has a range of an octave and a fourth and marking reduces it to a sixth. Van Morrison's recording of "Shenandoah" from *The Long Road Home* is a pop version of this traditional song.

Example 8.1

ELEMENTS OF VOCAL TECHNIQUE

95

THE CONTEMPORARY SINGER

"Shenandoah"

Example 8.2

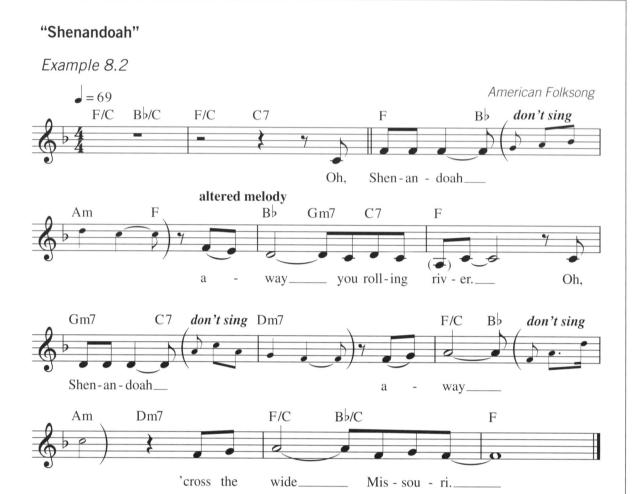

Marking example: "The Water Is Wide"

"The Water Is Wide" has a range of an octave while marking reduces it to a sixth. James Taylor's recording of "The Water Is Wide" from *New Moon Shine* may be of interest to you. Pay special attention to the way he rhythmically embellishes this song. This recording is a good study in vocal embellishments in a pop style.

Example 8.3

"The Water Is Wide"

Example 8.4

Learning to keep your voice healthy is an important part of your studies. If you take care of your instrument and follow common sense, you will stay healthy and sing well.

BREATH MANAGEMENT, resonant tone, registration, and articulation are interconnected parts of the overall process of singing. A great performance is an integration of these actions, where they occur almost simultaneously. Working to make them automatic should be the goal of aspiring singers.

ELEMENTS OF GOOD SINGING

1. Intake and management of air
2. Tone production
3. Articulation
4. Expression of ideas and emotions

Vibrato

Vibrato is the regular pulsing or oscillation of a single pitch produced by an alternating current of nerve impulses transmitted to the muscles of the larynx.

Combined with efficient breath management and a feeling of relaxation in the neck, jaw, and tongue muscles, these nerve impulses allow vibrato to occur.

Certain variations in speed and width of vibrato are considered to be normal. Normal speeds range from six to eight pulses per second, with much faster oscillation (bleat or tremolo) caused by excessive tension or manipulation of the laryngeal muscles. Slower, wide oscillations of a semitone or more in pitch, result in a wobble that can be caused by a lack of adequate breath support or by pulsing the abdominal muscles. Irregular vibrato pulsation can be caused by fatigue, poor breath support, unnecessary pressure added to singing, or vocal fold injury.

Straight tone, tone without any vibrato, is used in many different styles of music. While vibrato can add dimension and color and is considered to be a sign of free vocal production, being able to add and subtract vibrato can be a great asset in singing popular music.

If you lack vibrato and want to develop it, be sure not to force it. Most singers will develop vibrato if the other aspects of their singing are functioning well. Pleasant vibrato is dependent upon the balance of energy and relaxation in the breath management process. It will develop when your voice is ready, sometimes before adolescence, sometimes after, and should not be forced.

If you are curious about what vibrato feels like, work on exercises that induce light, flexible movement. You can also try to experiment by saying with a dramatic flair at a moderately high pitch level, "I'm a ghost!" Draw out the word ghost and let your voice shake a bit, making a ghostly sound. Try to remember the feeling of letting your voice go and see if that relaxed feeling can be transferred to singing the same words on single pitch. You might also try a trill, a rapid alternation between two pitches a half step apart. Repeat the following pattern moving up by half steps.

The following exercise is not what vibrato sounds like. It is an exercise to help you develop the freedom and flexibility to allow your natural vibrato to emerge.

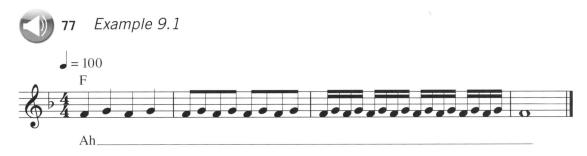

77   *Example 9.1*

Sustaining power

Being able to sustain a musical line gives you more interpretation and phrasing choices. In other words, you should be able to choose phrasing that fits the lyrics and shape of the musical line, rather than have it be dictated by lack of breath. Work to keep energized until the end of a musical line, and don't let your energy flag on descending phrases. In the following exercise, repeat the pattern moving up by half steps.

Flexibility and Sustaining Exercise

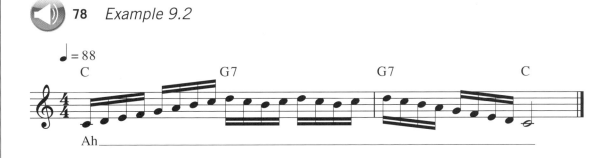

78   *Example 9.2*

Dynamics

You can use volume to vary the intensity of a song and add to its interpretation. In order to be able to sing well at loud and soft levels, you must have good breath support. Sing lightly in the middle of your range on the next exercise, repeating the pattern moving up by half steps.

Dynamic Flexibility and Control

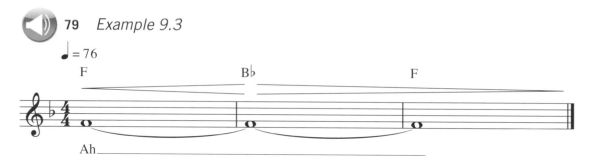

79 *Example 9.3*

Intonation

The ability to sing in tune is very important. Pitch problems are often related to excessive tension and/or breath control problems. For example, a singer who is singing flat might be lacking adequate breath energy or they might be using too much air pressure and over-blowing. Sharp singing can be caused by too much muscular tension or pushing. Vowels that are not clear can also affect intonation. When the singing process is coordinated—with adequate breath, proper registration, clearly pronounced vowels, and good emotional energy—it is more likely to be in tune.

Agility

Agility is important in singing melodic embellishments in gospel and much other popular music. Think of performances by Aretha Franklin, Stevie Wonder, and other popular artists. Agility requires freedom from muscular tension and reliance on steady air pressure. Working on a variety of melodic patterns can help you develop the ability to articulate fast runs of notes. Repeat the patterns moving up by half steps in the following exercises.

Minor Pattern 1

 80, 29 HIGH, 53 LOW *Example 9.4*

Minor Pattern 2

 81, 28 HIGH, 52 LOW *Example 9.5*

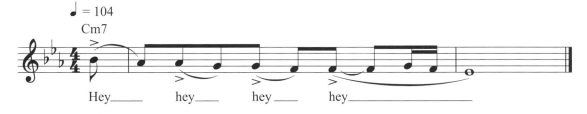

Minor Pentatonic Pattern

 82, 22 HIGH, 46 LOW *Example 9.6*

Pentatonic Triplets

 83, 27 HIGH, 51 LOW *Example 9.7a*

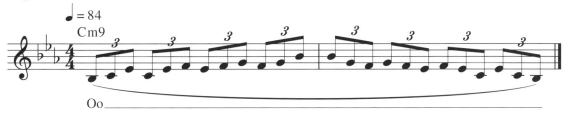

Alternate Rhythm Pentatonic Triplets

 84 *Example 9.7b*

Oo

Pentatonic Sixteenths

 85, 30 HIGH, 54 LOW *Example 9.8*

Ay(e)

Descending Minor Pentatonic Pattern

 86, 24 HIGH, 48 LOW *Example 9.9a*

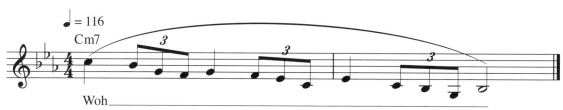

Woh

Ascending Minor Pentatonic Pattern

87, 25 HIGH, 49 LOW *Example 9.9b*

Woh

Voice Classification

Your voice can be classified according to several factors. Range and tone quality are the most important determining factors.

There are six basic voice types: soprano, mezzo-soprano, alto, tenor, baritone, and bass. Most young singers fit into one of these classifications, with the most prevalent voice types being soprano and baritone. It is important to note that the ranges in the voice classification chart are approximate and will vary depending on each individual's instrument and skill level.

The lowest female voice type is contralto, also referred to as "alto." The term "alto" is most commonly used in choral singing, describing the voice part below soprano and above tenor. In mixed choirs (men and women), lower-voiced women sing alto. In men's and boy's choirs, the alto part is sung by either adult male countertenors (the highest sub-classification for tenor voices) or by boys. Contralto is a voice classification used in classical singing to identify the lowest female voice type.

Belting is not a voice type, but rather a style of singing for women whose primary performing register is TA-dominant. Belters are often classified as either sopranos or mezzo-sopranos, but they sing in a TA-dominant style. The belter's range is included on the voice classification chart for your information.

Voice classifications

Bass

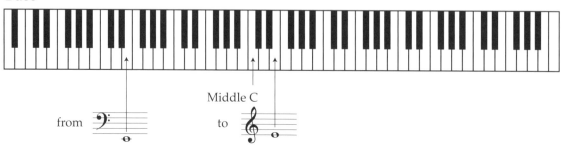

Baritone

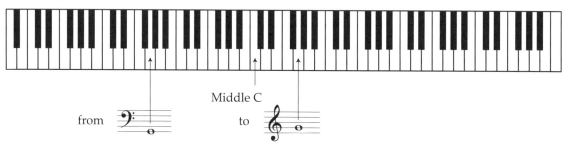

Tenor

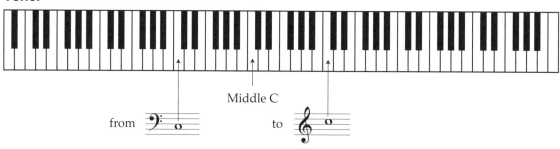

Alto (Contralto)

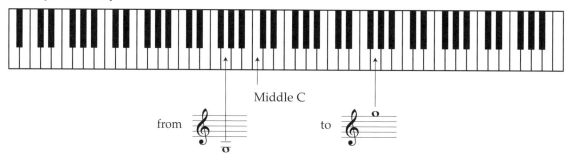

Mezzo - Soprano

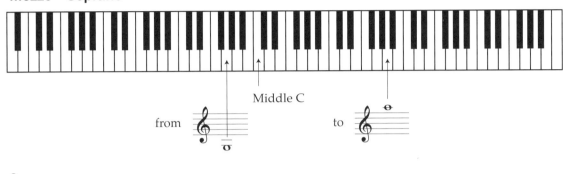

Soprano

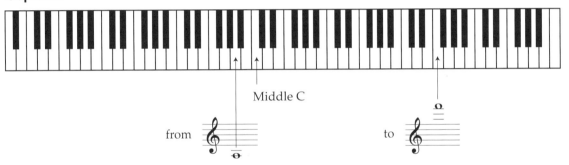

Belter Range

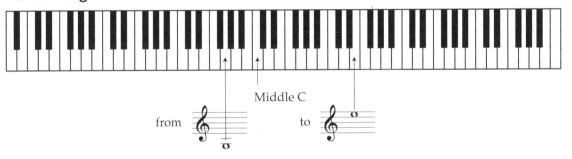

How to develop performing skills

It is valuable to practice performing for friends, family, and classmates to get a sense of how to direct your energy. You will gain experience and develop self-confidence by performing for an audience.

The size of your performing venue and the style of music you sing will dictate the size of your gestures and expressions. In a large auditorium, you can make larger gestures, move more, and fill the room with your energy. In a smaller venue, you can tone down the activity of your body, hands, and face, but keep the emotional energy level high.

In terms of style and depending on the venue, musical theater songs often require the performer to sing in character to portray the song. Jazz songs can have dramatic content too, but the style requires more subtle interpretation. You can learn a lot about performance technique by watching performers in a variety of styles. This will help you get a sense of what will work for you.

Understand a song's lyrics and find a way to empathize with its message or story. Tell the story. If you have trouble connecting with an audience, the following tips can help you begin to turn your focus away from self-consciousness and toward your music.

FOCUSING YOUR PERFORMANCE

Eyes

Many singers find it easier to sing for a large, anonymous audience in a concert hall than for a small audience in an intimate space. Discomfort seems to increase when singers are confronted with smaller performance space, and closer, watchful eyes. Although you might want to close your eyes to aid concentration and ward off self-consciousness, this can keep you from communicating with your audience. Try to keep your eyes open and focus outward to relate your song.

In a small space, try looking at your audience's foreheads or earlobes to give the sense you are directly looking at them without having to make eye contact. Don't look too high toward the back of the room. This may help you communicate your song.

Another technique is to find three focal points in the room. Looking straight out from center stage, envision 12 o'clock as directly behind the audience. For the

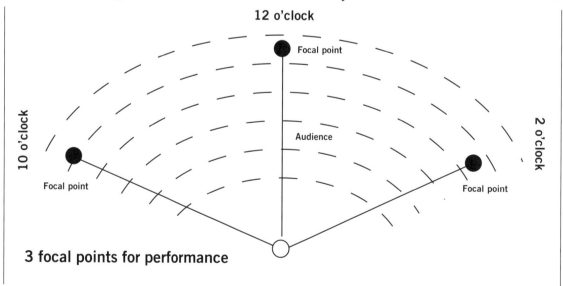

other two points, look toward 10 o'clock to your left and 2 o'clock to your right. Avoid constantly scanning the room while performing. Instead, shift your focal point based on the song's lyrics, or at changes in the form of the tune.

Hands

Gesture with your hands if you feel the urge. Some singers suddenly freeze and drop hand movement mid-stream when they become self-conscious. Try to follow through if you begin a gesture. Notice how you use your hands when you are speaking. Hand movement should be a natural offshoot of expressing yourself. Video-recording yourself will help you see what looks right for you.

Microphone technique is important in helping you get your best sound. It also gives you something to occupy your hands; however, don't fidget with the mic cord or wave it around in front of your mouth. Poor microphone technique detracts from your performance.

If you are accompanying yourself, don't let your playing detract from your singing. You should probably be more skilled on your accompanying instrument than you are as a singer. After all, you have to do two things at once, so you should be very proficient at both. Self-accompanied singers should be aware of posture to minimize tension and to maximize breath capacity.

CLASSICAL TO POP TRANSITION

Here are some ways classically-trained singers can get a better pop sound in their singing.

Vibrato

Singers often use less vibrato in popular music than in classical music, although some gospel and blues singers use a lot. Listen to singers in the style of popular music you like best, noting how much, how little, and when vibrato is used. Be aware of your vibrato and experiment with a straighter tone.

Diction

Modify formal diction to a more informal style of pronunciation. Depending on the style of popular music, you may need to pronounce lyrics more like everyday spoken language, in some cases even changing rhythms and phrasing to follow the natural accents in words.

Tone quality

Individuality is prized in popular music. The best tone for singing pop music is your natural voice enhanced by the skillful use of breath support and good diction. Be sure not to artificially darken your tone and that there is enough resonance in your tone to yield a balanced sound.

Volume

Most popular singers use microphones to amplify their voices to achieve balance with amplified instruments. Microphones make it possible for a singer with a small voice to be heard clearly. They have also made it possible to establish a more intimate style of singing ballads. Classical singers may need to scale back their volume to achieve a pop sound. Gain experience using a microphone so you can feel comfortable.

MICROPHONE TECHNIQUE

Microphones can be a great asset to singers. They also create fear in those who do not know how to use them, so some singers choose to avoid microphones and sound reinforcement altogether.

In contemporary music, however, you need to learn how to get a good sound with a microphone. How to achieve this can vary with performing venues, and it is an ongoing challenge for singers. Amplified sound is a part of many styles, and singers of popular music need to own a microphone and know how to set up to use it to their best advantage. It is also important for your vocal health when trying to project over an amplified band or even with a piano in a club. If you can't hear yourself due to a lack of amplification, you can over-sing and strain your voice.

A microphone can make you sound fuller and louder than you do naturally; however, it is not a substitute for vocal technique. By learning to sing you improve tone quality, flexibility, projection, expression, and more. Mics pick up and transmit everything, both good sound and bad. It is important to develop your voice to its fullest capacity so that the microphone serves as a tool, not a crutch.

In choosing which mic to purchase, consider your performing venue. Will you be singing in clubs where there is already a sound system you can plug in to? Are you joining a band that owns a sound system? Are you going to be in a recording studio where everything is set up? In all of these venues, you will need these basics.

- low-impedance microphone
- mic cable
- XLR-to-1/4 inch transformer

More elaborate set ups might also include:

- small amplifier with a 10" to 12" speaker
- digital reverb unit

Consider a basic model like the Shure SM58 for your first microphone purchase. It costs around $150 and will work in all kinds of live performance situations. Recording studios will have microphones for you to use, but you should have your own mic for performing anywhere else.

You will also need a heavy-duty microphone cable to connect your mic into the sound system. Most soundboards are set up to accept low-impedance mics (these have three small prongs in the mic base), but you should also purchase an XLR-to-1/4 inch transformer. This adapter makes it possible to connect a low-impedance mic into a guitar or keyboard amplifier that has a 1/4 inch plug.

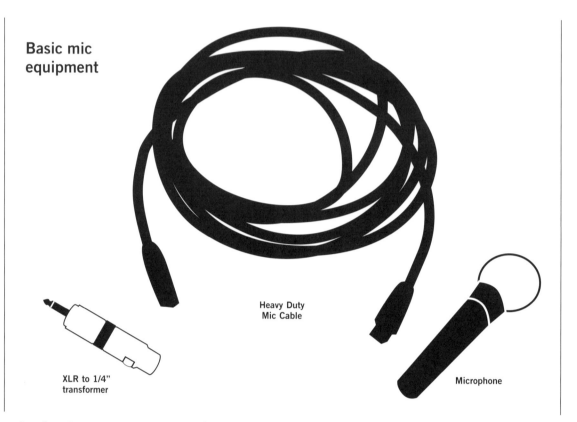

Basic mic equipment

Heavy Duty Mic Cable

XLR to 1/4" transformer

Microphone

After hooking up your microphone, position yourself so you can hear. Depending on the performance situation, you will probably need to hear your voice from a monitor, which is often angled up from the floor and pointed toward you. It will help you to know how loud you are singing, and keep you from blowing out your voice.

A problem with amplification is feedback, that all-too-familiar screeching sound you get sometimes when using a mic. Feedback results when the pickup range of your mic intersects with the amplified sound pattern of your speaker. To avoid this, don't point your mic at the speaker, and watch out for the feedback zone.

In rooms with a lot of hard surfaces such as concrete walls, linoleum, or hardwood floors, your voice may seem to bounce around the room, or reverberate, making it easy to hear yourself. This kind of a room is described as "live." Singers generally prefer them because it is easy to project and hear. You sound good singing in the shower because it is a good reverberation chamber. Rooms with upholstered furniture, carpet, and heavy curtains, on the other hand, absorb sound. If you sing in a "dead" room like this, you might feel your voice is being swallowed up, that you can't hear yourself, or that your voice has no carrying power.

You can also add effects to your sound electronically. The most basic effect is reverb, which makes an amplifier emulate the sound of a live room, making your voice sound fuller. This can keep you from pushing too hard for volume. The next best thing to singing in a live room is adding reverb from an amp or digital reverb unit. Too much reverb can make you sound like you're lost in a cave, so use it with discretion.

Most performing venues with a sound system will be able to add reverb to your vocal sound. If you want your own amp, a small one with a 10" to 12" speaker and built-in reverb can be purchased for around $250. There are many brands and prices, and a small practice amp can be useful for singers who regularly work with a rhythm section or band. You should be hooked into the main sound system with the band and also into your own amp so you can hear yourself. Even better than reverb built into your amp is connecting to an external digital reverb unit. It offers more control over the amount and quality of the sound you want and costs around $100.

THE CONTEMPORARY SINGER

118

ELEMENTS OF VOCAL TECHNIQUE

ADVICE FROM AN EXPERT

DONNA MCELROY, associate professor in the Voice Department at Berklee College of Music in Boston, is a professional singer with years of performing experience covering many styles of music. She offers the following advice:

How loud should you sing when using a microphone?

For ballads and sacred songs, treat the mic as if it were the ear of a dear loved one; a wonderful old person who'd given you some great advice. This evokes a different sound than if you were talking to a kid who's acting up in the supermarket. You would still be the same relative distance from the mic, but the intensity of volume and breath propulsion would be radically different, ranging from soft and very tender to the big voice of an angry or desperate cry. The well-adjusted, well-chosen mic will pick up the inflection or the intensity that is projected from the singer.

Can microphones enhance a weak voice?

Mics have been mischaracterized as a tool to provide body and presence for the vocalist. In my opinion, the mic should not be used as a crutch to provide these qualities. They should already be there and the mic should augment what the singer is already doing with his or her instrument. The projection a voice teacher drills into a singer's technique should be at its peak every time they sing so that sound personnel can get used to how this voice should be EQ'd.

How close and at what angle should a mic be held?

It depends on the mic, the song, the stage volume, the brand of mic, how close you want the mic to be—so many factors contribute to the efficiency of mic use. This takes time, so there should never be any one answer to this question. Flexibility and the ability to give maximum options to sound people is the key. It never hurts to ask these questions of the sound personnel testing your mic levels. The sound person might even change to a different mic, or set up two or three different brands of mics. If you get the sound you like, ask the sound person for the brand and model number of the mic.

In your opinion, what basic equipment should a singer have?

Until you have a record to sell or a known sound to re-emulate over and over, the singer only needs to have a mic, a cord, and an XLR adapter for plugging into the guitar or keyboard amp. It is nice to bring your own amp, but lots of times, there's an amp available at the gig. Before the gig, ask what you're expected to have. If you're just going to sit in, bring a mic-cord-XLR package.

PERFORMANCE ANXIETY

Many singers suffer nervousness or fear when performing. This anxiety manifests itself in many ways, including sweaty palms, dry mouth, too much saliva, and shaky knees. The interference and self-doubt that performance anxiety creates is very real for many singers. Here are some ideas to help you combat debilitating nervousness or even the lesser symptoms that keep you from singing your best.

Be prepared

Adequate preparation can go a long way toward offsetting the nervousness singers experience. If you know that you have not spent enough time studying the lyrics or memorizing the song, you can sabotage your own performance. It can take several weeks or months to get a song into your voice, mind, and body to the point you do not have to constantly focus on the next line or phrase. To reduce self-consciousness and self-doubt, allow enough time to thoroughly absorb the music before you perform.

Mental practice

Combat performance anxiety by eliminating negative thinking about your performance. Singers can mentally practice an entire performance to develop a sense of assurance, knowing what is going to happen and setting events moving in a positive direction. This can help control or eliminate negative thinking in performance. If you mentally practice one time for every three times you actually sing through your concert, you will be able to conserve vocal energy, correct errors, and sing with less anxiety (see Visualization in chapter 7).

Build a base of positive performing experiences

Plan to perform several times, over a period of months, for a friendly audience, with well-prepared music in a comfortable setting. Give yourself the opportunity to feel positive about your performances. If you do this repeatedly, and have a good experience, you may find that your confidence grows and you will be ready to branch out to other venues.

Breathing for relaxation

Since our voices are wind instruments, we need air to make them sound. The act of breathing also helps us get more oxygen to our brains and muscles to induce relaxation. Nervousness can make breathing shallow, and shallow breaths can create panic. This leads to more high breathing and the problem becomes circular.

Taking a few deep, relaxing breaths in preparation for performing can help. Don't hold your breath during instrumental introductions or during interludes. Include deep, relaxing breaths during your mental practice as well.

Avoid using alcohol to relax

Alcohol can help you lose your inhibitions, but it is much better to deal with your nervousness in a proactive way. Address your anxieties. Many vocalists find they are less nervous after they gain experience performing. Some need help from professionals who work with musicians in performance anxiety workshops. If you can't perform without alcohol, you should seek professional help.

Sounding "good"

Sometimes the overwhelming desire to sound good can get in a singer's way. This focus pulls our thinking inward too much, making it difficult or even impossible to be expressive. Wanting to sound good can make you start to focus on every little muscle movement or note. This kind of micromanaging is the death of spontaneous expression and lyrical singing. The bigger picture is lost to inward thinking and selfish control. If positive thinking is balanced with dedicated practice, you can relinquish conscious control and perform freely. As jazz pianist Kenny Werner writes in his book *Effortless Mastery*, "Technical mastery creates freedom."

It is very important to practice regularly with good focus. Stick with the task at hand, perhaps over a series of weeks or longer, until you have mastered it. It may take longer than one school semester. Vary your practice routine and find different ways to approach your challenges. Give yourself time to learn and grow.

Think when you practice. Then allow yourself time to turn off your mind and just sing. Repetition will teach your muscles to remember how to do the things you've been practicing. Then let go.

THERE ARE MANY different kinds of auditions, each with its own requirements. This text cannot address them all, but there are some universal guidelines that can help you to have a successful experience.

AUDITION GUIDELINES

Follow instructions

If the audition literature lists specific song requirements, be sure your material meets them. Many auditions require you to choose at least two songs in contrasting tempos, but always check. If there are no specific requirements, perform songs that show what you do best and display your uniqueness as a singer. This will set you apart from the crowd and may give you the edge you need to succeed.

Prepare

Auditions are not the time to try out new, untested material. Give yourself plenty of time to do a mock audition to test your material out a few times. Ask a friend to video-record you so you can self-correct before the actual audition. The more you know about what to expect, the more likely you will feel in control and not surprised, nervous, or flustered.

Memorize

Make sure that everything you plan to sing for an audition is memorized. In this regard, there are no exceptions. You must perform from memory.

Warm up

Always warm up before an audition. Your job is to present yourself at your best. Your best voice reveals itself after you have gotten the morning cobwebs out and your vocal engine is running smoothly. For an early morning audition, get a good night's sleep, wake up early, and warm up enough that you can sing freely right from the start of your audition. Warming up takes time. If you have an audition at 8 a.m., you should be up and humming gently or singing lightly by 6 a.m.

If you cannot warm up before you arrive because of travel time, or if you are unfamiliar with the audition site, call in advance and ask where you can warm up before your audition.

Arrive early

Arrive early to give yourself time to find the audition room, get settled, and focus on your music. A late arrival to an audition is very poor form. Always plan extra time to get where you need to be.

Accompaniment

Don't assume that there will be an accompanist provided. Find out if you should bring an accompaniment track or CD, and bring a portable player in case the audition room doesn't have one. You can also bring an mp3 player and adapter cord to plug into a sound system.

If an accompanist is provided, be courteous to them—it reflects badly on you if you treat them poorly. Tape separate pages of music together. This makes it easier for the accompanist to read and keeps them from getting out of order or falling off the piano.

Be prepared to count off the tempo for the accompanist. Practice this. If, when you begin, something sounds different than you expect, don't look accusingly at the pianist. Keep going unless everything is falling apart. If it is, stop, take a deep breath, count off the tempo, and begin again. Lead confidently and the accompanist will follow, even if you are wrong. If something doesn't go as expected, count it as a learning experience. Take responsibility for everything that happens in an audition.

Make sure your music is in the right key for you. Although some audition pianists are capable of transposing on sight, there is always the chance that they will make an error and compromise your audition. Your job is to present yourself at your best. Don't take the chance that someone else will jeopardize your audition.

Never ask an accompanist to transpose your audition song to a different key in an audition or any other performance situation.

Good preparation of materials gives an accompanist a better shot at supporting you and making your audition successful. Also, ask if you will need to bring sheet music with written-out accompaniment, or a lead sheet with chord changes.

Musical selection

Choose music that meets the audition requirements, sheet music or a legible chord chart, displays the best qualities of your singing, is not overly long, and is reasonably easy to play.

A cappella pieces are not recommended unless you have perfect pitch. Even then, they may not be the best choice for an audition, as the audition team can benefit from hearing you interact with accompaniment. If it is appropriate for the style of music you are singing, edit out long instrumental interludes in your audition pieces.

Some auditions call for a 16-bar-long excerpt of your music. This is often used at large open auditions or "cattle calls" where hundreds of singers audition for one or two jobs, and need to be heard in a short time. Your 16-bar cut should include your best singing, perhaps displaying your high range. Work this out in advance of the audition.

What to wear

Dress for the occasion. If you have a formal audition, dress accordingly but be comfortable enough to breathe. It is important to be comfortable for less formal auditions too, but it helps to look like you put some effort into your appearance. Many singers perform better if they are well dressed because they feel better about the way they look. Practice your audition in the clothes you plan to wear so the feeling of new or unfamiliar clothes and shoes doesn't distract you.

Performing skills

Your movement and gestures should be appropriate for the size of the audition space and style of music. Smaller rooms require less movement, larger rooms may need a bit more. Always be sincere and be yourself. Focus your eyes on the auditioners' foreheads or earlobes so you don't corner them into looking directly into your eyes. This can be uncomfortable for you and for the audition team.

After you sing

After you are finished singing, you may ask when you can expect to hear the results if you don't know. But other than that, keep your exit simple. Say "thank you," smile, pick up your music, and leave. Asking auditioners how you did as soon as you are finished is not recommended. People who audition usually have a full day of continuous listening scheduled. They will be better able to evaluate your audition given the time to discuss their impressions and put their thoughts into writing.

I HAVE SELECTED THREE CLASSIC songs for you to practice singing: a pop ballad, a medium-swing jazz tune, and a medium- to up-tempo Motown song.

"YESTERDAY"

Many singers, including Ray Charles, En Vogue, Boyz II Men, and Michael Bolton, have recorded this classic pop ballad first sung by Paul McCartney. The original key would be appropriate for high-voiced male singers. Men who sing this song in the original key should have an easy high F in order to sing the middle section freely and without tension. Women and lower voiced men who sing "Yesterday" may prefer to use the lower key of C to get a nice pop sound. The high E and F in the higher key can be difficult for some women to sing lightly and without too much vibrato. If you have trouble singing them with a straighter tone, choose the lower key.

This song has a wide range of ten notes and can be challenging in terms of range and expression. When performing pop songs, work to strike a balance between singing expressively and being subtle. A lot of hand movement or melodramatic facial expressions do not enhance this song. Strive to be sincere and draw upon your own emotional experience to make the song appropriately genuine and heartfelt.

Yesterday (key of F)

Words and Music by John Lennon
and Paul McCartney

Yesterday (key of C)

"I'M BEGINNING TO SEE THE LIGHT"

My favorite recording of this song is by Ella Fitzgerald on her *Duke Ellington Songbook* recording. Ella sings it in the key of C, which is fairly low for most women. But after she sings the song once through as written, she masterfully embellishes to create her own variation of the song, which extends up quite high. If singers start with the melody too high, there is no room for embellishment above the melody.

Women who sing this song in the key of C should sing an octave lower than the melody is written. If the melody were written where it is sung, all the notes would need ledger lines. It is much more practical to notate it on the staff. Singers who feel more comfortable singing higher can use the key of G, singing the notes on the staff as written.

I'm Beginning to
See the Light (key of C)

Words and Music by Don George, Johnny Hodges,
Duke Ellington and Harry James

THE CONTEMPORARY SINGER

132

ELEMENTS OF VOCAL TECHNIQUE

I'm Beginning to See the Light (key of G)

Words and Music by Don George, Johnny Hodges, Duke Ellington and Harry James

"I HEARD IT THROUGH THE GRAPEVINE"

Marvin Gaye sings the most famous version of this song, although Gladys Knight and the Pips and many others have also recorded it. The Gladys Knight and the Pips version features a different melody and it is interesting to observe the lyric changes she makes. Marvin Gaye's version is used here, with alternate lyrics included for a female singer.

Men should observe the use of falsetto in Marvin Gaye's recording of the highest notes and experiment with this in their singing. This falsetto effect can be achieved with practice, and by making your voice lighter.

I Heard It Through the Grapevine (key of E♭ minor)

Words and Music by Norman J. Whitfield
and Barrett Strong

Interlude

D.S. al Coda

2. I know a man ain't supposed to cry,
   Take a good look at these tears in my eyes
   Baby, but these tears I can't hold inside.
   Losin' you would end my life, you see,
   'Cause you mean that much to me.
   You could have told me yourself
   That you loved someone else.
       Instead, I heard it through the
       grapevine *(etc.)*

3. People say believe half of what you see,
   Son, and none of what you hear,
   But I can't help bein' confused.
   If it's true please tell me, dear.
   Do you plan to let me go
   For the other guy (girl) you loved before?
   Don't you know,
       I heard it through the grapevine *(etc.)*

ELEMENTS OF VOCAL TECHNIQUE

THE CONTEMPORARY SINGER

I Heard It Through the Grapevine (key of C minor)

*Words and Music by Norman J. Whitfield
and Barrett Strong*

D.S. al Coda

3. Peo-ple say be-lieve half_

_ it through the grape-vine, not much   long - er would you be   my   ba -

Hon-ey, hon-ey   I   know__

(etc. to end)

by,   Yeah,_ yeah,   yeah,_ yeah,   Heard_

that you're let-tin' me go,_____   Said I   heard_____ it through the grape-vine,

fade and repeat

Ooh,_   I   heard_   it through the grape-vine,   Ooh, noo, I   heard_

. I know a man ain't supposed to cry,
  ake a good look at these tears in my eyes
  aby , but these tears I can't hold inside.
  osin' you would end my life, you see,
  'Cause you mean that much to me.
  You could have told me yourself
  hat you lo ved someone else.
          Instead, I heard it through the
       grapevine *(etc.)*

3. People say believe half of what you see,
   Son, and none of what you hear,
   ut I can' t help bein' confused.
   If it's true please tell me, dear.
   o you plan to let me go
   For the other guy (girl) you loved before
   on 't you know,
          I heard it through the grapevine *(etc.)*

THE BASIC VOWEL sounds are represented here in several languages. Two of the word examples in English are not pure vowels, but rather, diphthongs. They are indicated as diphthongs by symbol (d) next to the word.

BASIC ENGLISH WITH FOREIGN LANGUAGE VOWELS

Vowel	English	Italian	German	French	Japanese
ee	weak	si	sie	hiver	いいじま
ih	hit		immer		（イとエの中間 - エの口でイを言う）
ay	day (d)	vero	leben	été	えい
eh	met	belle	denn	clair	エプロン
ah	father	casa	Mann	ras	スカ二ト
aw	crawl	gloria	kommt	folie	（アとオの中間 - アの口でオを言う）
oh	tone (d)	dove	so	hôtel	におう（匂う）
oo	clue	piu	Du		ゆううつ

There are several specific vowel sounds not listed above that are characteristic of English. They are found with many different spellings, some of which are listed below. Nonnative English speakers may need to concentrate on these in order to be understood when singing and speaking English.

VOWEL SOUND	ENGLISH WORD
er	earth, girl, world
	(minimize Rs before consonants)
uh	much, but, young, love, does, flood
short u	put, full, good, woman, would
short a	mash, flat, cat, grab
short i	hit, rely, women, busy, bitter

PRONUNCIATION PRACTICE

Here is a list of words and phrases that can be challenging to non-native speakers of English. Many of these words focus on the pronunciation of R and L as well as difficult links between words. Try creating phrases with these ordinary words and practice them daily.

Usually	Remembering	Industrial	Experience
Unusually	Literate	Published	Admiration
River	Lovely	Lyrics	Friendly
Would	Little	Material	Freely
Reality	Illiterate	Recording	Dreams
Severity	Literacy	Criminally	Dreamily
Deliberate	Probably	Ceremonially	Thrilling
Million	Release	Miraculous	Thrills
Trillion	Believable	Miraculously	
Really	Absolutely	Marvelous	
Rarely	Industry	Illusion	

Will you still love me?

I've wanted it desperately.

These are tough wounds to heal.

The very thought of you thrills me.

I've been running through the wilderness.

Red leather, yellow leather.

I would freely urge the fellow to apply.

You drive me crazy.

You went through with it.

I believe that you would be unfaithful.

The night was like a thousand others.

The toothless old thing filled her mouth with moss.

A trillion stars illuminate Riley's miraculous flight.

The yellow thread creates an illusion that runs through the material.

The circumference of the remaining area will provide ample room for the

caterers to construct their forty-layer tiramisu!

BEGINNING WARM-UP FOR ALL VOICES

Performance Note: Change vowels and syllables to suit your voice on the scales and exercise patterns.

Descending Fifth / Lip Trill-Slide

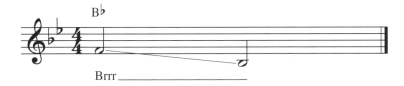

THE CONTEMPORARY SINGER | ELEMENTS OF VOCAL TECHNIQUE

Fifth Slide and Octave Slide, Liptrill and Oo

5-Note Descending Pattern

Major Triad Pattern

5-Note Descending Pattern

Skipping Thirds Pattern

Descending Thirds Pattern

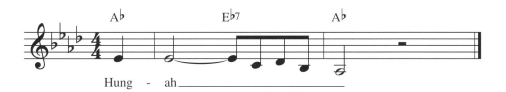

LEVEL 1 WORKOUT

Major/Minor Triplets

High Range

9 HIGH

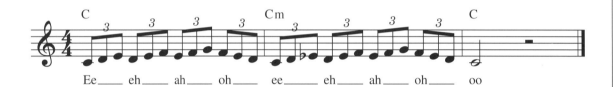

Ee___ eh___ ah___ oh___ ee___ eh___ ah___ oh___ oo

Low Range

33 LOW

Ee___ eh___ ah___ oh___ ee___ eh___ ah___ oh___ oo

Three 5-Note Scales

High Range

10
HIGH

Low Range

34
LOW

Descending Intervals

High Range

Low Range

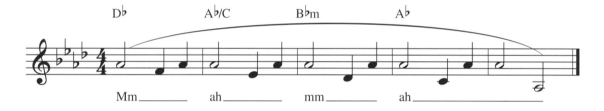

9-Note Scale

High Range

12 HIGH

Ah

Low Range

36 LOW

Ee

Octave Arpeggio

13 HIGH High Range

See_____ ah_____

37 LOW Low Range

Ee_____

Descending Triplets

High Range

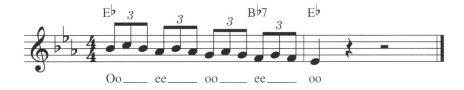

Oo_____ ee_____ oo_____ ee_____ oo

Low Range

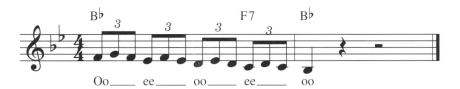

Oo_____ ee_____ oo_____ ee_____ oo

3-, 5-, and 9-Note Scales

High Range

15
HIGH

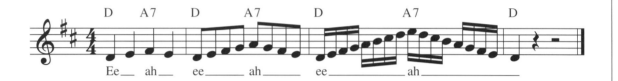

Low Range

39
LOW

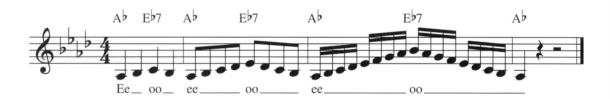

Single-Tone Pattern

High Range

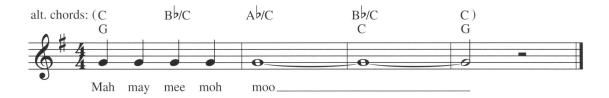

alt. chords: (C   B♭/C   A♭/C   B♭/C   C)
        G   C   G

Mah   may   mee   moh   moo_____

Low Range

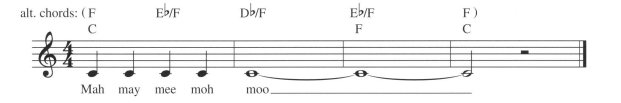

alt. chords: (F   E♭/F   D♭/F   E♭/F   F)
        C   F   C

Mah   may   mee   moh   moo_____

Descending Sixteenth Pattern

High Range

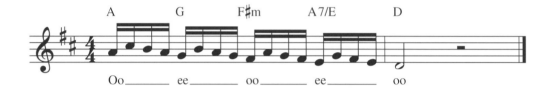

A   G   F#m   A7/E   D

Oo_____ ee_____ oo_____ ee_____ oo

Low Range

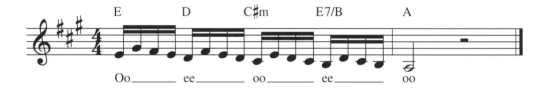

E   D   C#m   E7/B   A

Oo_____ ee_____ oo_____ ee_____ oo

Octave Arpeggio with Turn and Descending Scale

High Range

18 HIGH

Ee_____ oo_____ ee___ ah_____

Low Range

42 LOW

Ee_____ oo_____ ee___ ah_____

ELEMENTS OF VOCAL TECHNIQUE

157

THE CONTEMPORARY SINGER

Legato-Staccato Pattern

High Range

19 HIGH

Oo

Low Range

43 LOW

Ee

Humpty Dumpty Etude

High Range

Hump - ty Dump - ty sat on a wall, Hump - ty Dump - ty had a great fall.

All the king's hors - es and all the king's men could - n't put Hump-ty to - geth - er a - gain.

All the king's hors - es and all the king's men could - n't put Hump - ty to - geth - er a - gain.

Low Range

Hump - ty Dump - ty sat on a wall, Hump - ty Dump - ty had a great fall.

All the king's hors - es and all the king's men could - n't put Hump - ty to - geth - er a - gain.

All the king's hors - es and all the king's men could - n't put Hump-ty to - geth - er a - gain.

ADVANCED WORKOUT

Octave Arpeggio with Added Seventh

High Range

Low Range

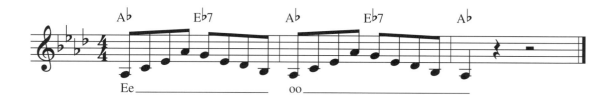

Minor Pentatonic Pattern

High Range

22
HIGH

Woh_____ yeah__ yeah_____

Low Range

46
LOW

Woh_____ yeah__ yeah_____

Descending Triplets Octave

High Range

23
HIGH

D   G   D   A7   D

Oo_____ ee_____ oo_____ ee_____   oo_____ ee_____ oo_____ ee

Low Range

47
LOW

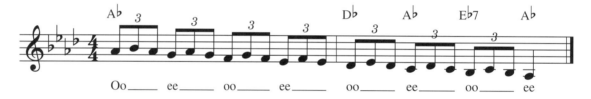

A♭   D♭   A♭   E♭7   A♭

Oo_____ ee_____ oo_____ ee_____   oo_____ ee_____ oo_____ ee

Descending Minor Pentatonic Pattern

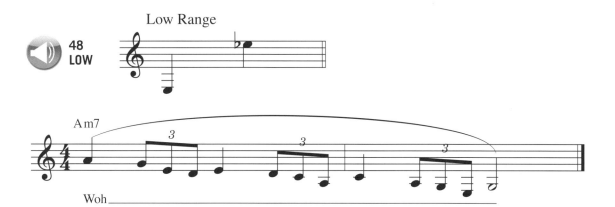

ELEMENTS OF VOCAL TECHNIQUE

THE CONTEMPORARY SINGER

Ascending Minor Pentatonic Pattern

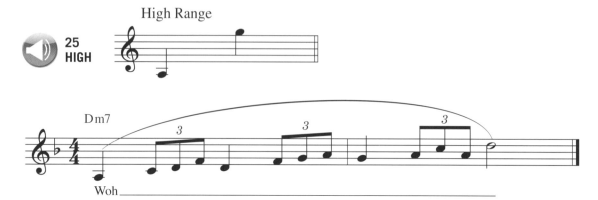

5-, 9-, 11-Note Scales with Descending Arpeggio

Minor Pentatonic Triplets

High Range

27
HIGH

Ah

Low Range

51
LOW

Oo_____ ee_____ oo_____ ee_____ oo_____ ee_____ oo_____ ee_____

Minor Pentatonic Pattern

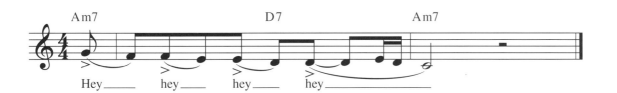

Minor Pattern

High Range

Low Range

Pentatonic Sixteenths

High Range

30 HIGH

Em7

Ee

Low Range

54 LOW

Cm7

Ee

Legato Arpeggio

High Range

31 HIGH

Low Range

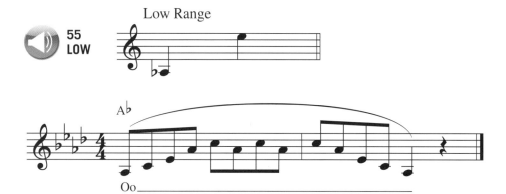

55 LOW

Interval Steps

High Range

32 HIGH

Low Range

56 LOW

Abdomen: The portion of the body lying between the pelvis and chest (not including the back) that houses the majority of the digestive organs.

Adam's apple: The protruding aspect of the thyroid cartilage in the front of the neck, which is more prominently visible in males.

Alto: The lowest female voice type, also known as "contralto." The term alto is also commonly used in choral singing to refer to the voice part below soprano and above tenor.

Articulation: The process of producing consonants in speech and singing.

Articulators: The parts of the mouth involved in the creation of sounds for speech and singing.

Arytenoid cartilages: The two pyramid shaped cartilages to which the vocal folds are attached. Primarily, they control the position and tension of the vocal folds during phonation and breathing.

Aspirate: A speech sound characterized by air preceding the onset of tone, sounds like the letter H.

Aspiration: In speech, the sound of air preceding or following vocal fold vibration; in medicine, when a foreign object, or the contents of the stomach (as in reflux) is sucked into the lungs. Aspiration can lead to lung infection.

Attack: The beginning of vocal fold vibration in response to airflow. See Onset.

Belting: A TA-dominant style of singing where the lower register is mixed upward to make a loud, emotional, full sound. Belting is sometimes used in musical theater, blues, rock, and pop singing.

Breath management: The efficient process of breathing used in singing.

Bass: The lowest of male voice types.

Baritone: The most common male voice type, higher than bass and lower than tenor.

Bulimia: An illness involving self-induced vomiting to control weight.

Cartilage: The connective tissue characterized by firm consistency. It is softer and more flexible than bone and relatively nonvascular in nature.

Catch breath: A quick breath taken to renew air supply, not indicated by a rest in music.

Chest resonance: The sensation of vibration felt in the lower throat and upper chest areas of the body when singing or speaking. Chest resonance originates in the lower pharynx rather than the chest. It can be felt more easily when singing at a lower pitch level, or at a high volume.

Chest voice/register: A commonly used term for the lower register of a voice, named for the sensations of vibrations in the chest. Also referred to as heavy mechanism, low register, and thyroarytenoid dominant or TA dominant.

Cricoid cartilage: The lower circular cartilage of the larynx attaching the larynx to the trachea (windpipe).

Cricothyroid muscles: The CT muscles are responsible for lengthening and thinning the vocal folds. The resulting sound is commonly known as "head voice" for women and "falsetto" for men.

Cricothyroid dominant: CT-dominant vocal production is commonly known as "head voice" for women and "falsetto" for men.

Consonant: A speech sound created by interrupting the flow of air with articulating organs.

Contralto: The lowest female voice type, also called alto. The term contralto is most commonly used in operatic voice typing. Alto is commonly used in choral singing to refer to the voice part below soprano and above tenor.

Diaphragm: The large double-dome shaped muscle that separates the chest from the abdominal cavity, and which facilitates the breathing process.

Diphthong: A double vowel occurring in a single syllable (e.g., my = mah + ee).

Diction: The formation and delivery of words according to established principles of pronunciation.

Dynamics: The aspect of music referring to relative loudness or softness in musical performance.

Edema: The excessive accumulation of fluid in tissues; swelling.

Embellishment: The ornamentation of a melody, adding notes above and below it or changing the existing rhythm of a song to enhance interpretation.

Epiglottis: The leaf-shaped cartilage flap that covers the glottal opening, which helps keep food out of the larynx.

Exhalation: The part of the breathing cycle when the air is expelled from the lungs.

Expression: The interpretation of mood, feeling, and intent in music. It also refers to the physical aspect and involvement of interpretation (e.g., facial expression).

Falsetto: The highest, lightest register of the male voice, produced by a crico-thyroid-dominant muscle action.

Flexibility: The ability of the voice to make rapid adjustments in pitch, dynamics, and to move with agility over a series of pitches.

Flute voice/register: The highest register of a female voice marked by a whistle-like quality. It is also referred to as an upper extension, whistle tone, flageolet. Flute voice is cricothyroid-dominant.

Forward resonance: A desirable sensation of the voice vibrating in the mask.

Fundamental tone: The basic sound produced by the vibrating vocal folds.

Focus: A sense of concentrated vocal energy resulting in a clear, efficient tone quality.

Glottal attack: The onset of tone occurring on words beginning with vowels. Breath pressure is built up under closed vocal folds, then quickly released either harshly or gently.

Glottis: The space between the vocal folds.

Groove: A continuous rhythmic pattern used in songs to establish style and feel.

Hard attack: See Glottal attack.

Hard palate: The bony portion of the roof of the mouth.

Head resonance: A sensation of vibration in the area of the forehead when singing in a higher register. Head resonance is thought to origi-nate in the upper pharynx and mouth rather than the head. It can be more easily felt when singing at a higher pitch level.

Head voice/register: A commonly used term for the higher register of a voice, with sensations of vibrations in the head. In women's voices, it is produced by a cricothyroid-dominant action. In men's voices, "head voice" is sometimes used to describe a pre-falsetto mix.

Hyoid bone: A U-shaped bone located at the top of the larynx.

Hum: A vocal sound made with closed lips.

Inhalation: The part of the breathing cycle when air is taken into the lungs.

Intonation: Singing or playing in tune.

Improvisation: Spontaneous melodic and rhythmic invention.

Intercostals: The muscles between the ribs.

Imagery: The use of words to create mental pictures or images that illustrate vocal concepts.

Laryngitis: An inflammatory condition of the larynx. Can be caused by illness, smoking, or vocal misuse.

Larynx (Voice box): An organ at the top of the trachea composed of bone, cartilage, ligaments, and muscles and membranes. It contains the vocal folds, which are closed during phonation and swallowing and open during breathing.

Legato: Smooth and connected.

Mask: The area of the eyes, nose, cheeks, upper lip, and teeth, which has a sensation of vibration while singing.

Middle voice/register: The middle register of a voice with sensations of vibrations in the mask, and head. Also referred to as medium, blended, or mixed register.

Mezzo-soprano: A female voice type with a range just slightly lower than a soprano.

Nodules (Nodes): Callous-like growths on the vocal folds, usually resulting from vocal misuse.

Onset: The beginning of vocal fold vibration in response to airflow. See Attack.

Oscillation: Repeated movement back and forth.

Open chest voice: Loud, forceful singing in the lowest vocal register for women. If open chest voice is over-used and/or pushed up high in range, vocal strain or damage may occur.

Otolaryngologist: An ear, nose and throat doctor.

Overtones: The upper harmonics that result from the fundamental tone setting air in the human resonating system in motion.

Palate: The roof of the mouth in two parts, hard and soft.

Passaggio: The transitional passage or bridge between vocal registers.

Pharynx: The region above the larynx that extends from behind the nasal cavity to the gateway to the esophagus.

Phonation: In singing, the vibration of the vocal folds, which produces sound.

Polyp: A mass that can grow on the vocal folds as a result of various kinds of abuse, including smoking and screaming; typically the result of recurrent vocal hemorrhage (bleeding).

Range: The total scope of notes that one can sing.

Reflux: A backflow of stomach contents into the esophagus and throat that causes inflammation, hoarseness, chronic coughing, a feeling of fullness, a lump in the throat, and increased mucus production.

Register: The term used to designate a portion of the vocal range in which the notes have a similar tone quality and are produced by the same muscle action.

Resonance: The intensification of a fundamental tone through sympathetic vibration.

Resonator: The surfaces or air containing cavities that vibrate in response to a fundamental tone.

Riffing: Improvised melodic embellishment.

Scatting: Melodic and rhythmic vocal improvisation using nonsense syllables (scat syllables), which are imitative of musical instruments.

Soft palate: The roof of the mouth behind the hard palate; it is flexible and muscular.

Staccato: Short, separate articulation of notes.

Sternum: The breastbone, in the center of the chest, to which the ribs attach.

Straight tone: A tone without vibrato.

Timbre: Tone color.

Thyroid cartilage (Adam's apple): The largest cartilage of the larynx.

Thyroarytenoid muscles: The TA muscles are responsible for shortening and thickening the vocal folds. The resulting sound is commonly known as "chest voice."

Thyroarytenoid dominant: TA-dominant vocal production is commonly known as "chest voice."

Trachea (Windpipe): A cartilaginous tube through which air passes to the lungs.

Trill: The rapid alternation of two adjacent pitches.

Unvoiced consonant: A consonant articulated without vocal fold vibration (e.g., P, H, F, S, K).

Vamp: An accompaniment pattern repeated until the soloist begins to sing or play.

Vibrato: An oscillation of tone above and below a pitch center produced by alternating nerve impulses.

Vocal coach: A professional who works with singers, specializing in teaching repertoire, language pronunciation, style, and performance.

Vocal folds: Two muscular folds formed by the thyroarytenoid muscles, capable of closing over the windpipe and vibrating in response to air pressure from the lungs, resulting in vocal tone. They open during breathing and close during phonation and swallowing.

Vocal fry: A vocal sound sometimes referred to as "glottal fry" because of the grating sound made when insufficient air pressure is used for vocalization.

Vocal tract: The resonating system comprised of the larynx, pharynx, and the mouth cavity.

Vocalise: A vocal exercise designed to achieve specific objective(s).

Vocalize: To sing a melody or scale pattern on a vowel sound, sometimes for the purpose of warming up.

Voice teacher: A professional who teaches singing technique. May also act as a Vocal coach. (see Vocal coach)

Voiced consonant: A consonant articulated with vocal fold vibration (e.g., Z, V, G, B).

Vowel: A speech sound produced when breath is not interrupted (e.g., ee, ay, oo, oh, ah).

Vowel modification: The vowel adjustments made to allow for tone equalization when singing at higher pitch levels.

WEB SITES

■ **The Voice Foundation**

www.voicefoundation.org

Informative site with information on the singer's voice, speaker's voice, and voice problems.

■ **Texas Voice Center**

texasvoicecenter.com/diseases.html

Pictures of healthy and unhealthy vocal folds.

■ **National Center for Voice and Speech**

www.ncvs.org/e-learning/index.html

A good source for voice information.

■ **Mark Baxter Vocal Studios**

www.voicelesson.com

Voice teacher Mark Baxter explores topics of interest to singers, with an emphasis on pop and rock singing.

BOOKS

Alderson, Richard. **Complete Handbook of Voice Training.** West Nyack, NY: *Parker Publishing, 1979.*

Balk, Wesley. **The Complete Singing Actor.** Minneapolis: *University of Minnesota Press, 1977.*

Green, B. with W.T. Galwey. **The Inner Game of Music.** Garden City, NY: *Doubleday, Anchor Press, 1986.*

Lessac, A. **The Use and Training of the Human Voice** (revised). Mountain View, CA: *Mayfield Publishing Company, 1967.*

Linklater, Kristen. **Freeing the Natural Voice.** New York: *Drama Book Specialists, 1976.*

McClosky, D.B. **Your Voice at Its Best.** Plymouth, MA: *Memorial Press, 1972.*

McKinney, J. **The Diagnosis and Correction of Vocal Faults.** Nashville, TN: *Genovex Music Group, 1994.*

Miller, Richard **The Structure of Singing.** London: Schirmer Books, *Collier MacMillan Publishing, 1986.*

Sataloff, R.T. **Vocal Health and Pedagogy.** San Diego, London: *Singular Publishing Group, Inc., 1998.*

Ungerleider, S. **Mental Training for Peak Performance.** Emmaus, PA: *Rodale Press, Inc., 1996.*

Werner, K. **Effortless Mastery.** New Albany, IN: *Jamey Aebersold Publishing, 1996.*

MUSIC

American Folk Songs and Spirituals. Milwaukee, WI: *Hal Leonard Corporation, 1996.*

The Beatles Fake Book. Milwaukee, WI: *Hal Leonard Corporation, 1987.*

Classic Rock Fake Book (revised). Milwaukee, WI: *Hal Leonard Corporation, 1996.*

The Definitive Country Collection. Milwaukee, WI: *Hal Leonard Corporation, 1992.*

Mantooth, F. **The Best Chord Changes for the World's Greatest Standards.** Milwaukee, WI: *Hal Leonard Corporation, 1989.*

Mantooth, F. **The Best Chord Changes for the Most Requested Standards.** Milwaukee, WI: *Hal Leonard Corporation, 1990.*

Sher, Chuck. **Latin Real Book (vocal).** Petaluma, CA: *Chuck Sher Publishing, 1997.*

Sher, Chuck. **The New Real Book, Vols. 1, 2, and 3 (vocal).** Petaluma, CA: *Chuck Sher Publishing, 1984 and 1995.*

Walters, R., ed. **The Singers Musical Theater Anthology.** (4 vols. each for soprano, mezzo soprano/belter, tenor, baritone/bass, and duets). Milwaukee, WI: *Hal Leonard Corporation, 1987.*

The Ultimate Pop/Rock Fake Book. Milwaukee, WI: *Hal Leonard Corporation, April, 1997.*

Ultimate Gospel (revised). Milwaukee, WI: *Hal Leonard Corporation, August, 1983.*

About the Author

ANNE PECKHAM is a singer, voice teacher, and author. A professor in the Voice Department at Berklee College of Music, her work as a teacher and her publications have influenced popular singing pedagogy worldwide. Her approach embraces the foundations of good vocal technique, while building singers' skills in jazz, pop, and rock music.

At Berklee, in addition to teaching private voice lessons, she continues to develop curricular materials for *Elements of Vocal Technique*, a required course for all of Berklee's 700 vocal students. Her work at the college, including Berklee's Musical Theater Workshop and the Berklee Concert Choir, has helped enrich the musical experience of thousands of students over the years. Alumni of Anne's classes and lessons include many professionals in the music industry.

Anne is the author of four publications for Berklee Press: *The Contemporary Singer* and its companion *Vocal Workouts for the Contemporary Singer* (both released in Japanese translations), *The Singer's Handbook* from the Berklee in the Pocket series, and *Vocal Technique: Developing Your Voice for Performance*, an instructional DVD.

As a member of the National Association of Teachers of Singing, Anne served as vice president on the Boston chapter's board of directors. She has traveled extensively as a vocal clinician and adjudicator for song and choral festivals in North America, South America, and Europe. Her master classes and vocal pedagogy seminars for students and teachers focus on approaches to rock, jazz, pop, and r&b music.

Anne sang with the Tanglewood Festival Chorus for four years, performing on two recordings with the Boston Pops, including a featured solo in their televised Gilbert and Sullivan presentation, which aired on PBS. She has performed with regional theater companies, has worked as a professional soloist with area church choirs, and performs frequently in recital and cabaret venues. She also recently appeared as a voice coach on both the PBS children's show *Fetch!* and on the TV reality series *Trial by Choir*.

Index

Note: Page numbers in *italics* indicate illustrations.

More Fine Publications

Berklee Press

GUITAR

BEBOP GUITAR SOLOS
by Michael Kaplan
00121703 Book $16.99

BLUES GUITAR TECHNIQUE
by Michael Williams
50449623 Book/Online Audio..........$24.99

BERKLEE GUITAR CHORD DICTIONARY
by Rick Peckham
50449546 Jazz – Book $12.99
50449596 Rock – Book $12.99

BERKLEE GUITAR STYLE STUDIES
by Jim Kelly
00200377 Book/Online Media..........$24.99

CLASSICAL TECHNIQUE FOR THE MODERN GUITARIST
by Kim Perlak
00148781 Book/Online Audio.............$19.99

CONTEMPORARY JAZZ GUITAR SOLOS
by Michael Kaplan
00143596 Book........................$16.99

CREATIVE CHORDAL HARMONY FOR GUITAR
by Mick Goodrick and Tim Miller
50449613 Book/Online Audio.............$19.99

FUNK/R&B GUITAR
by Thaddeus Hogarth
50449569 Book/Online Audio...........$19.99

GUITAR SWEEP PICKING
by Joe Stump
00151223 Book/Online Audio $19.99

INTRODUCTION TO JAZZ GUITAR
by Jane Miller
00125041 Book/Online Audio.............$19.99

JAZZ GUITAR FRETBOARD NAVIGATION
by Mark White
00154107 Book/Online Audio.............$19.99

JAZZ SWING GUITAR
by Jon Wheatley
00139935 Book/Online Audio.............$19.99

METAL GUITAR CHOP SHOP
by Joe Stump
50449601 Book/Online Audio $19.99

A MODERN METHOD FOR GUITAR – VOLUMES 1-3 COMPLETE*
by William Leavitt
00292990 Book/Online Media $49.99
*Individual volumes, media options, and supporting songbooks available.

A MODERN METHOD FOR GUITAR SCALES
by Larry Baione
00199318 Book............................$10.99

READING STUDIES FOR GUITAR
by William Leavitt
50449490 Book.........................$16.99

Berklee Press publications feature material developed at the Berklee College of Music.
To browse the complete Berklee Press Catalog, go to
www.berkleepress.com

BASS

BERKLEE JAZZ BASS
by Rich Appleman, Whit Browne & Bruce Gertz
50449636 Book/Online Audio...........$19.99

CHORD STUDIES FOR ELECTRIC BASS
by Rich Appleman & Joseph Viola
50449750 Book $17.99

FINGERSTYLE FUNK BASS LINES
by Joe Santerre
50449542 Book/Online Audio...........$19.99

FUNK BASS FILLS
by Anthony Vitti
50449608 Book/Online Audio...........$19.99

INSTANT BASS
by Danny Morris
50449502 Book/CD................................$9.99

METAL BASS LINES
by David Marvuglio
00122465 Book/Online Audio.............$19.99

READING CONTEMPORARY ELECTRIC BASS
by Rich Appleman
50449770 Book..........................$19.99

ROCK BASS LINES
by Joe Santerre
50449478 Book/Online Audio...........$22.99

PIANO/KEYBOARD

BERKLEE JAZZ KEYBOARD HARMONY
by Suzanna Sifter
00138874 Book/Online Audio $24.99

BERKLEE JAZZ PIANO
by Ray Santisi
50448047 Book/Online Audio $19.99

BERKLEE JAZZ STANDARDS FOR SOLO PIANO
arr. Robert Christopherson, Hey Rim Jeon, Ross Ramsay, Tim Ray
00160482 Book/Online Audio $19.99

CHORD-SCALE IMPROVISATION FOR KEYBOARD
by Ross Ramsay
50449597 Book/CD $19.99

CONTEMPORARY PIANO TECHNIQUE
by Stephany Tiernan
50449545 Book/DVD...........................$29.99

HAMMOND ORGAN COMPLETE
by Dave Limina
00237801 Book/Online Audio............$24.99

JAZZ PIANO COMPING
by Suzanne Davis
50449614 Book/Online Audio.............$19.99

LATIN JAZZ PIANO IMPROVISATION
by Rebecca Cline
50449649 Book/Online Audio $24.99

PIANO ESSENTIALS
by Ross Ramsay
50448046 Book/Online Audio $24.99

SOLO JAZZ PIANO
by Neil Olmstead
50449641 Book/Online Audio..........$39.99

DRUMS

BEGINNING DJEMBE
by Michael Markus & Joe Galeota
00148210 Book/Online Video.............$16.99

BERKLEE JAZZ DRUMS
by Casey Scheuerell
50449612 Book/Online Audio.............$19.99

DRUM SET WARM-UPS
by Rod Morgenstein
50449465 Book...........................$12.99

A MANUAL FOR THE MODERN DRUMMER
by Alan Dawson & Don DeMichael
50449560 Book...........................$14.99

MASTERING THE ART OF BRUSHES
by Jon Hazilla
50449459 Book/Online Audio...........$19.99

PHRASING
by Russ Gold
00120209 Book/Online Media $19.99

WORLD JAZZ DRUMMING
by Mark Walker
50449568 Book/CD $22.99

BERKLEE PRACTICE METHOD

GET YOUR BAND TOGETHER
With additional volumes for other instruments, plus a teacher's guide.
Bass
by Rich Appleman, John Repucci and the Berklee Faculty
50449427 Book/CD $19.99
Drum Set
by Ron Savage, Casey Scheuerell and the Berklee Faculty
50449429 Book/CD $14.95
Guitar
by Larry Baione and the Berklee Faculty
50449426 Book/CD $19.99
Keyboard
by Russell Hoffmann, Paul Schmeling and the Berklee Faculty
50449428 Book/Online Audio............$14.99

VOICE

BELTING
by Jeannie Gagné
00124984 Book/Online Media.............$19.99

THE CONTEMPORARY SINGER
by Anne Peckham
50449595 Book/Online Audio...........$24.99

JAZZ VOCAL IMPROVISATION
by Mili Bermejo
00159290 Book/Online Audio.............$19.99

TIPS FOR SINGERS
by Carolyn Wilkins
50449557 Book/CD $19.95

VOCAL WORKOUTS FOR THE CONTEMPORARY SINGER
by Anne Peckham
50448044 Book/Online Audio..........$24.99

YOUR SINGING VOICE
by Jeannie Gagné
50449619 Book/Online Audio............$29.99

WOODWINDS & BRASS

TRUMPET SOUND EFFECTS
by Craig Pederson & Ueli Dörig
00121626 Book/Online Audio...........$14.99

SAXOPHONE SOUND EFFECTS
by Ueli Dörig
50449628 Book/Online Audio..........$15.99

THE TECHNIQUE OF THE FLUTE
by Joseph Viola
00214012 Book...$19.99

STRINGS/ROOTS MUSIC

BERKLEE HARP
by Felice Pomeranz
00144263 Book/Online Audio...........$19.99

BEYOND BLUEGRASS BANJO
by Dave Hollander and Matt Glaser
50449610 Book/CD..............................$19.99

BEYOND BLUEGRASS MANDOLIN
by John McGann and Matt Glaser
50449609 Book/CD..............................$19.99

BLUEGRASS FIDDLE & BEYOND
by Matt Glaser
50449602 Book/CD..............................$19.99

CONTEMPORARY CELLO ETUDES
by Mike Block
00159292 Book/Online Audio...........$19.99

EXPLORING CLASSICAL MANDOLIN
by August Watters
00125040 Book/Online Media.........$22.99

THE IRISH CELLO BOOK
by Liz Davis Maxfield
50449652 Book/Online Audio.........$24.99

JAZZ UKULELE
by Abe Lagrimas, Jr.
00121624 Book/Online Audio...........$19.99

AUTOBIOGRAPHY

LEARNING TO LISTEN: THE JAZZ JOURNEY OF GARY BURTON
by Gary Burton
00117798 Book...$27.99

MUSIC THEORY, EAR TRAINING & IMPROVISATION

BEGINNING EAR TRAINING
by Gilson Schachnik
50449548 Book/Online Audio..........$16.99

BERKLEE BOOK OF JAZZ HARMONY
by Joe Mulholland & Tom Hojnacki
00113755 Book/Online Audio............$27.50

BERKLEE MUSIC THEORY
by Paul Schmeling
50449615 Book 1/Online Audio.......$24.99
50449616 Book 2/Online Audio......$22.99

CONTEMPORARY COUNTERPOINT
by Beth Denisch
00147050 Book/Online Audio.........$22.99

IMPROVISATION FOR CLASSICAL MUSICIANS
by Eugene Friesen with Wendy M. Friesen
50449637 Book/CD.............................$24.99

REHARMONIZATION TECHNIQUES
by Randy Felts
50449496 Book.......................................$29.99

MUSIC BUSINESS

CROWDFUNDING FOR MUSICIANS
by Laser Malena-Webber
00285092 Book.......................................$17.99

ENGAGING THE CONCERT AUDIENCE
by David Wallace
00244532 Book/Online Media.........$16.99

HOW TO GET A JOB IN THE MUSIC INDUSTRY
by Keith Hatschek with Breanne Beseda
00130699 Book.......................................$27.99

MAKING MUSIC MAKE MONEY
by Eric Beall
50448009 Book.....................................$29.99

MUSIC INDUSTRY FORMS
by Jonathan Feist
00121814 Book.......................................$15.99

MUSIC LAW IN THE DIGITAL AGE
by Allen Bargfrede
00148196 Book.......................................$19.99

MUSIC MARKETING
by Mike King
50449588 Book.......................................$24.99

PROJECT MANAGEMENT FOR MUSICIANS
by Jonathan Feist
50449659 Book.......................................$29.99

THE SELF-PROMOTING MUSICIAN
by Peter Spellman
00119607 Book.......................................$24.99

MUSIC PRODUCTION & ENGINEERING

AUDIO MASTERING
by Jonathan Wyner
50449581 Book/CD..............................$29.99

AUDIO POST PRODUCTION
by Mark Cross
50449627 Book.......................................$19.99

CREATING COMMERCIAL MUSIC
by Peter Bell
00278535 Book/Online Media.........$19.99

THE SINGER-SONGWRITER'S GUIDE TO RECORDING IN THE HOME STUDIO
by Shane Adams
00148211 Book.......................................$16.99

UNDERSTANDING AUDIO
by Daniel M. Thompson
00148197 Book.......................................$34.99

WELLNESS

MANAGE YOUR STRESS AND PAIN THROUGH MUSIC
by Dr. Suzanne B. Hanser and Dr. Susan E. Mandel
50449592 Book/CD $29.99

MUSICIAN'S YOGA
by Mia Olson
50449587 Book.......................................$19.99

THE NEW MUSIC THERAPIST'S HANDBOOK
by Dr. Suzanne B. Hanser
00279325 Book.......................................$29.99

Prices subject to change without notice. Visit your local music dealer or bookstore, or go to **www.berkleepress.com**

SONGWRITING, COMPOSING, ARRANGING & CONDUCTING

ARRANGING FOR HORNS
by Jerry Gates
00121625 Book/Online Audio............$19.99

BEGINNING SONGWRITING
by Andrea Stolpe with Jan Stolpe
00138503 Book/Online Audio...........$19.99

BERKLEE CONTEMPORARY MUSIC NOTATION
by Jonathan Feist
00202547 Book.......................................$19.99

COMPLETE GUIDE TO FILM SCORING
by Richard Davis
50449607 Book.......................................$29.99

CONDUCTING MUSIC TODAY
by Bruce Hangen
00237719 Book/Online Media..........$24.99

CONTEMPORARY COUNTERPOINT: THEORY & APPLICATION
by Beth Denisch
00147050 Book/Online Audio.........$22.99

THE CRAFT OF SONGWRITING
by Scarlet Keys
00159283 Book/Online Audio...........$19.99

CREATIVE STRATEGIES IN FILM SCORING
by Ben Newhouse
00242911 Book/Online Media...........$24.99

JAZZ COMPOSITION
by Ted Pease
50448000 Book/Online Audio $39.99

MELODY IN SONGWRITING
by Jack Perricone
50449419 Book.......................................$24.99

MODERN JAZZ VOICINGS
by Ted Pease and Ken Pullig
50449485 Book/Online Audio.........$24.99

MUSIC COMPOSITION FOR FILM AND TELEVISION
by Lalo Schifrin
50449604 Book.......................................$34.99

MUSIC NOTATION
by Mark McGrain
50449399 Book.......................................$24.99
by Matthew Nicholl and Richard Grudzinski
50449540 Book.......................................$19.99

POPULAR LYRIC WRITING
by Andrea Stolpe
50449553 Book.......................................$15.99

THE SONGWRITER'S WORKSHOP
by Jimmy Kachulis
Harmony
50449519 Book/Online Audio $29.99
Melody
50449518 Book/Online Audio $24.99

SONGWRITING: ESSENTIAL GUIDE
by Pat Pattison
Lyric and Form Structure
50481582 Book.......................................$16.99
Rhyming
00124366 Book.......................................$17.99

SONGWRITING IN PRACTICE
by Mark Simos
00244545 Book.......................................$16.99

SONGWRITING STRATEGIES
by Mark Simos
50449621 Book.......................................$24.99

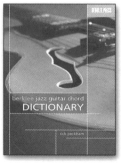
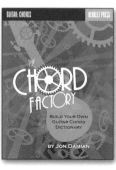

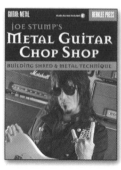
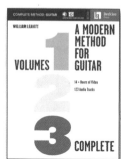